# Natural Alternatives
## for You and Your Home

**175 recipes to make eco-friendly products**

**Casey Kellar**

**krause publications**
*A subsidiary of F+W Media, Inc.*

**700 East State Street • Iola, WI 54990-0001**
**715-445-2214 • 888-457-2873**
**www.krausebooks.com**

Our toll-free number to place an order or obtain
a free catalog is (800) 258-0929.

*Neither the author nor Krause Publications assumes any liability for uses made of the metric information presented. All units are approximate.*

*Neither the author nor Krause Publications can be held responsible for any injuries, losses, or other damages resulting from the use of information in this book (due to different conditions, tools, and individual skills); however, great care has been taken to ensure that the information in this book is accurate.*

Library of Congress Control Number: 2008941158

ISBN-13: 978-1-4402-0241-4
ISBN-10: 1-4402-0241-9

Cover photography by Kris Kandler

Designed by Donna Mummery
Edited by Candy Wiza

Printed in China

*Mission statement: Enjoy the simple things in life while you reduce, reuse and recycle.*

# DEDICATION

In remembrance of my family who have gone before me — a talented group of "DIYers" — who have played an important role in shaping my life and with love to all who follow.

To you the reader, for your family's enrichment, knowledge, pleasure and cost savings. The information in this book is a combination of knowledge handed down from my own family and the experience gained in my years as a natural chemical designer. Enjoy!

# ACKNOWLEDGMENTS

I would like to thank the following for their support and expertise:

My husband, Byron, who always willingly sets aside his tasks to assist me so I can write.

My daughter, Nicole, who is my faithful sounding board and cheerful helper.

Krause Publications, for their help and patience, especially, Candy Wiza, editor; Heidi Zastrow, designer; and Kris Kandler, photographer.

# TABLE OF CONTENTS

Easy to Make – Environmentally Friendly – Cost Saving!!!

# INTRODUCTION

*Having is sometimes not as sweet as the wanting — Simple is better — Less is more!*

My dear reader, whether you are just starting out in your new home, apartment or dorm or if you live with an abundance of stuff you've accumulated over the years, my goal is to help you save money and time and provide you with healthy alternatives. Read this book, take action, and you will make a difference in yourself and the environment.

These recipes don't take a lot of time and the packaging can be simple or complex, depending on your personal or gifting needs. It's all very simple once you get the hang of it. You'll get examples of savings throughout the book and plenty of helpful hints.

In the wake of concerns about product safety, our future in the face of an uncertain economy where it is becoming harder and harder to make ends meet and with the effects of global warming, this book's purpose is simple and direct — learn how to make changes in your life for your health, make a difference in this world of declining resources and save money in the process!

My Dad used to say, "Every penny is a solider. Add them up and it will give you an army against hunger." No matter what age or stage of life you're in, I believe this same principle applies today. Every little change we make in our lives to make it simpler, better and more enjoyable, every little environmental change we make towards preserving and restoring, every little thing we do to save money and become more efficient is like a little "soldier" in a war turning the tide on a world declining in resources.

Thinking economically is not being cheap; it's being economically sound, allowing you to use your finances in areas that are most important to you. Thinking environmentally is not being radical; it's being responsible. I know if you have bought this book and you're reading it, I am probably preaching to the choir, but thank you for allowing me the indulgence of my platform. I am deeply committed as I'm sure you are too.

Little things done by a mass of people can affect a huge change. Consider this — when you buy store-bought goods, a large amount of what you are paying for is the packaging and marketing of that product, plus all the retailer's mark-ups along the way. Not paying for these enhancements alone will save you money. Also, consider the length of time an item sits on the shelf before being purchased and how many preservatives must be added to prolong its shelf life.

When making these recipes, you are going to avoid adding a long list of preservatives and you'll have fresh products. Plus, you'll know exactly how old the product is. After you make your product, place on a label (you can add graphics to your labels using a computer) and write the name and make date on it, you'll have control of your own products at a huge discount. Most big discount retailers would make you pay an extra cost for the savings. This book represents a one-stop shopping center in the form of a guide with no annual renewal fee.

My goal is to inspire you to make changes for yourself, your pocketbook, your family, the environment and for fun and relaxation. Before you know it, these simple lifestyle changes will become second nature to you. Enjoy working from this book and recommend it to others. Together, we can make a difference in your health and our world.

Because of my commitment to sustainability, I am donating two percent of my net proceeds from the sales of this book to planting and reforestation. Two percent may not sound like a lot, but what if everyone did this with money they earned? If we all do a little toward improving our health and home space, save money and resources, contribute back to the environment and solve hunger, what a better place this would be for all of us.

You don't have to create all the cost-saving recipes in this book (I would love it if you did) but start with just one or two and start to improve your life by getting back in control. Then, when that becomes routine, refer back to this book and add a few more. It doesn't have to be overwhelming. Do a project with your family, make a gift box or share a few recipes with someone. Affect change this way and everyone benefits.

My best regards to you. I hope you enjoy reading this book as much as I enjoyed writing it for you.

*Casey*

# START RIGHT WITH SIMPLE AND HEALTHY LIVING

Before we start, we need to talk about life. If you purchased this book, you are probably looking for a way to live simply, longer and healthier and you want to be in control of your living environment, health and beauty products. Good for you! Now, sit down on that chair or on your bed and let me talk to you for a minute....

There is no single, great secret to good health and happiness. We are bombarded with advertising from the health, beauty and home goods industries offering instant solutions, a "cure-all," or the promise that a specific item, if used, will make you better, more peaceful, etc. If you find you are lethargic, have a lack of vitality or generally feel tired and your doctor cannot determine what it is, it may be lack of exercise or sleep, poor diet, or not enough relaxation time. You cannot get total long-lasting health and vitality from a pill or magic mix.

Peace and total health of the mind and body come from (and I know you've heard this before) the everyday function of caring for yourself. We'll call it a lifetime plan for health and well-being. It is what you feed your mind and body and what you do each and every day to take care of yourself. This amazing health prescription for life is not a quick fix, but rather a lifetime plan.

## LEARN AND EXPLORE

Everyday learn a little something — like a child. Look for wonder in the small things around you. Explore your passions, your hobbies or means of recreation that feed your very spirit. I know it seems like the world is spinning faster and faster, but you can make the time, even if it is only 15 minutes out of the day.

## GET OUT OF YOUR CHAIR!

Optimum exercise time is at least 45 minutes, four days a week. Even on your busiest days, find 15 minutes to stand up and stretch, wiggle or jump around. When you get the blood flowing to your brain, you'll be more productive, make up the time lost and you'll be a little healthier — no excuses.

Fatigue and a range of illnesses often are the result of a lack of exercise. When you exercise, you get increased breathing and an elevated heart rate which help a change occur on a cellular level. Oxygen-starved cells can cause fatigue from a lack of exercise. Also, there is that real advantage of "letting off steam" that happens when you provide an outlet for your "fight and flight" response. You will be happier and healthier if you move your body everyday. Take it from "Mom;" get some fresh air and exercise and you will feel a whole lot better.

# YOU ARE WHAT YOU EAT

Eating good food is part of the lifetime plan. I realize all my readers come from different backgrounds with an assortment of cultural foods and beliefs, so I will keep this brief and give you some simple words of advice that will crossover and help almost all of you, despite your diet habits or beliefs.

White sugar and white flour have very little nutritional value. If it is not functional for you to eliminate them from your diet completely (although I think that's a good idea) at least control the amount you consume.

Establish a balanced diet (whole grains, fruits, vegetables, lean proteins and calcium-rich foods) and eat more often during the day but in small amounts. Breakfast is important, and it's better if you do not eat after 7:00 p.m. so that your body can rest during its natural "fasting" time.

Doing the activities above will help keep your weight at a healthy place and the need for any kind of a future diet will be greatly minimized. Fresh, clean, whole foods and raw foods in a balanced diet contain all the nutrients your body needs to properly assimilate and use the minerals and vitamins contained in the foods. For safety reasons, you may need to cook meats and fish, but fresh, washed raw fruits and vegetables are stellar for your health, so eat your veggies. You want to be beautiful or handsome; it all starts from the inside out.

When we talk about food, almost always the word diet comes up. Let's talk about dieting for a minute. Pretend you've been through a time of great celebration, holidays or a stressful schedule that has caused you to put on a few pounds (I know the world throws us some curves at times). What do we do?

Once I was at a lecture and the speaker said to the audience, "when it comes to losing weight, I have a special secret. It works every time and it is easy to do and easy to remember, so I cannot believe there are so many overweight people in the world. Would you like me to tell you what it is?" "Yes, yes," the people in the audience yelled, "tell us your secret." There was a long dramatic pause....The speaker smiled wisely and simply said, "move more; eat less."

Well, it is simple and it is guaranteed to work, so why do we refuse to do what we KNOW will work instead of buying high-priced products (we don't know what they are chemically doing to our body) or pay huge amounts for specialty foods? Here it is kids, straight and true.... Move more; eat less. How's that for simple and better. Use a salad plate instead of a dinner plate for your four small meals (you will burn more calories eating four small meals a day). Drink plenty of fluids to move the toxins out of your body, and fit in any type of exercise to your day. Guess what? THIS WORKS, and it allows your body do adjust itself naturally.

# WATER — THE ELIXIR OF LIFE

Drink six to eight glasses a day. (Four is a minimum; more is better within reason.) Known to eliminate toxins, ward off infections and clear up skin, we cannot live without it. Fluids containing caffeine and alcohol do not count as your daily water intake. I used to think that this was hard to do, but you get to count liquids in soups and other liquid items combined with foods, so this is not as difficult as you might think.

## LAUGHTER IS GOOD MEDICINE

Spending time with family and/or friends actually will help you live longer. Take time to get together once in awhile and share your week, your thoughts, and listen to theirs. Make sure you choose the "right" friends. The "right" friends are positive people who have things in common with you and they're heading their lives in a good direction. With good friends and good family relations, you can prevent sitting on a "shrink's" couch and move forward feeling happy and supported. You deserve this. If you do not have a natural supportive family, remember, family is who you surround yourself with. Friends can be like family if you develop the right ones, and friendship is a two-way street, so treat others as you want to be treated and all should go well.

Sad, but true, my life was so busy that I had to add time in my schedule for fun. I highly recommend doing this if you have a busy lifestyle. Make a list of things you like to do for fun: swim, play cards with friends, go out for dinner and a movie, dance, play golf, spend a quiet night at the library, go to a spa, etc. Whatever the things are that you love, but you're not fitting into your life, add to your to-do list. It's sad that we live in such a fast-paced world that we have to schedule this in our lives. You know what they say about all work and no play (if you don't – "oops," you're a workaholic!).

## REST

Just as good water, food and exercise are basic to our health, so is rest. Too often in our lives we hurry around, stressed out, don't eat right and think we are too busy to get enough rest, but rest is probably what you need the most during these times.

You need between six and eight hours of sleep (varies by person and stress level) for your brain and body to be fully recharged and rested. Learn to say no to those extra activities and late nights. You will function much better if you have the vitality and energy needed to draw upon for your work and fun activities during the day. If you are rested, you also will be able to think better on your feet and handle that stressful situation much better. A sleep-deprived nervous system is its own little hell in life, so take care of your mind, body and nervous system. Your family and co-workers will thank you for it.

Having trouble sleeping? There are some insomnia remedies on page 108. But if you develop a little pre-bedtime wind-down ritual such as cutting back on caffeine and alcohol, taking a warm bath or reading something in the evening, you will find that you can train yourself to trigger a "sleep response" habit in no time.

# FOLLOW YOUR HEART AND YOUR PASSIONS

A wise person once said, "do what you love and the money will follow." It is true that when you are doing something you love, time just flies, and work can seem like play if you are following your passion or dream. If you are one of the lucky ones who can turn what you love into a career, than I applaud you. If you are not, make sure you develop a hobby or activity that you can do on a regular basis that gives you that sense of fulfillment. Also, if you work for someone else, it is important, along with punching the clock, that you take time to find out what it is in your job that really contributes to the "whole" of the purpose or the company. It is so important that we all realize what we do is important. It gives our life meaning and completes our purpose on this planet. Take a few moments, get a piece of paper and pen, and do this little drill.

Write down your various "hats" across the top of the paper. For example:

| Mom | (Job Title or Career Title) | Wife | Little League Coach |
|-----|------------------------------|------|---------------------|
|     |                              |      |                     |
|     |                              |      |                     |
|     |                              |      |                     |
|     |                              |      |                     |

Under each of the headings, make notes of what you do in each category that makes a difference, makes someone's life better, fills a service or gives something back to you.

Why? Because the goal is to do things with passion, do them well and with purpose. How can you feel fulfilled unless you have a good understanding of how you are contributing, what you are contributing and how you feel about that contribution?

If you have trouble coming up with the reasons, ask your boss or a family member how or what you can do to make a bigger impact. You may be surprised at how much you actually contribute at home and at work. It is important to our very souls to have a feeling that we contribute and that our lives have meaning. You will be amazed at how your feelings of self-worth grow. Also, how can you contribute in the most effective ways if you do not understand your purpose?

# ELIMINATE EXCESS STRESS

Some stress in our lives is natural, some we learn and grow from and some is just unavoidable. There are many different kinds of stress: a first date, meeting your in-laws for the first time, moving, a death of a good friend or family member, etc. However, we can take control of some stress. Some temporary stresses are good; some are bad and they just happen; it's a part of life. More damaging is long-term (chronic) stress that can severely compromise your health. Long-term stress from an abusive family member, the wrong job or a similar situation can be overwhelming, as it has no relief or recovery time in between. Chronic stress can lead to anxiety, long-term emotional imbalance and even physical illness. You must learn when to make the necessary changes in your life to protect yourself and when to just say NO. Learn to prioritize what you want in your life, where you can dedicate time and what you simply can't do.

Once, one of my adult children had a tough decision to make and came to me, not to make the decision, but to ask for counsel as to how to get through the process. Through my own experience, the best tool I ever learned came from my father. I will share it with you in case you ever need it.

## The Ben Franklin Decision List

It was told to me that when Ben Franklin had to make a decision, he would make a list to help him evaluate his process. It is very simple and effective.

Using the table, under the FOR heading, write all the positive things about the situation that you can think of; just let your mind and heart wander. Under the AGAINST heading, write all the negative reasons or things about the situation. Take some time with the list and sleep on it; you may find yourself adding to one side or the other.

My father said that when Ben Franklin would look at his list and one side was much longer than the other, he knew how to vote or what decision he should make. Give it a try when faced with something difficult; it will make things a lot clearer for you.

I've offered some good basics for living to put into practice. Now, start working your way through all the products you can make for yourself, your families and pets and your home environment. Learn to save money and live a simpler and healthier life!

| FOR (the positives) | AGAINST (the negatives) |
|---|---|
|  |  |
|  |  |
|  |  |
|  |  |

# INGREDIENTS, EQUIPMENT, COST AND EFFORT

This book is intended to be, as the title reminds us, a guide to simple-to-make, easy-to-use items to help you save money and the environment. All the items in this book (unless otherwise noted in the recipe) can be found at most grocery, health food, hardware or pharmacy stores. Many times, if it is an ingredient or product that a store could carry and chose not to, most store managers will special order an item for you if you ask.

For mixing, most of the items will be standard things you have in your home. It is prudent to note, however, that sometimes plastic can alter and absorb strong odors and certain metals can alter essential oils and some ingredients.

I recommend mixing most of the products in either glass bowls or stainless steel, as these are the most dependable.

The equipment includes stainless steel or glass mixing bowls, measuring cups and measuring spoons, cutting board, double boiler, eyedroppers (glass are best), knives, kitchen scale, grater, mortar and pestle, peeler, shakers and sifter. A high-powered food processor or a Vita Mix™ will be helpful, but not mandatory for any of these recipes.

Most of the products are for personal use only, but there are a few products suitable for "making into a business," as some people have discovered from my previous books.

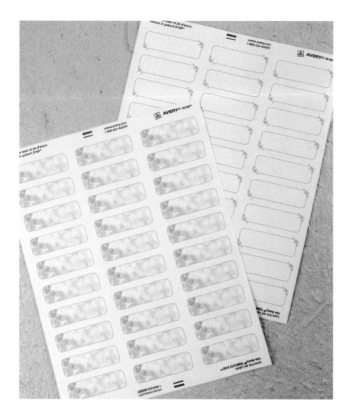

## LABELING

Labeling is important, whether it is for your home use or gift giving. Many of the recipes will note a shelf life. Remember to label your creations so you know when the shelf life expires. I have given you conservative shelf life dates in this book. Some recipes actually may last longer, but since I have no control over the storage conditions or packaging, I have made the dating conservative.

## PACKAGING

Many of the products do not require special packaging; however, having several sizes of plastic and glass storage containers and labels accessible will make storing your latest creation a breeze. When you make your own products, you most likely will be using recycled containers, or if you buy new containers, refill them over and over. A huge amount of what you are paying for when you buy store-bought goods is the packaging and marketing of that product. Plus, all the retailers add their mark-ups along the way. Not paying for these conveniences will save you a lot of money.

Keep a watchful eye out for gift-style containers and embellishments such as pretty bottles, tins, boxes, lace, ribbon, fabric, etc., so that you have a small reserve available for storing your personal cost-saving creations. Purchase blank labels and use your computer to make pretty handmade labels, or buy cute "made in the kitchen of" labels and use colored pens to write in your gift information. Scrapbooking supply Web sites and stores have some great items for labeling and decorating your gift items.

When using recycled containers, cleanliness is an important issue. Your safe and natural product will not stay that way if you use a container that is not properly cleaned and sterile. Make sure if you are using a recycled container (also a good idea for new containers) to clean it thoroughly with hot soapy water, then rinse well to remove any soap residue. The upper rack in most dishwashers and a hot water setting will be sufficient. Arrange containers upside down so they get the best cleaning results.

## STORAGE

These products should be stored in a cool dark place or in the refrigerator. The shelf life is indicated under the recipe and noted by a span of time. Why the time span? The shelf life is partially dependent on climate factors. With hot humid climate/conditions, expect a shorter shelf life; cooler drier climate/conditions can increase the shelf life.

# CHAPTER ONE

# PERSONAL CARE FOR YOU AND THE ONES YOU LOVE

# BEAUTIFUL SKIN IS IN

Radiant, beautiful skin can be yours cheaper than you thought and without irritating, harsh additives or scary-sounding ingredients. In a world full of synthetics, being able to whip up nutrient-rich formulas for beautiful skin right in your own kitchen and save money is easier than you thought.

Cleanse, tone and moisturize your skin at least two times a day. Once in the morning to cleanse away any oils and dead skin that has accumulated during the night and to prep your skin for the day. (Your skin needs cleaning and breakfast just like you.) Then again at night to remove free radicals, make-up, dirt trapped by oils, etc. The secret is to gently clean and not over-strip the skin.

## BASIC SKIN TYPES

Before choosing which product to make for yourself, stand in front of a mirror and determine your skin type, such as dry, oily or normal skin. The following descriptions will help you determine what products are right for you and your skin type.

**Dry Skin**

Dry skin usually feels tight or dry and flaky because it lacks moisture. People with dry skin may be young, but more likely to be over 40 and have lines around the eyes and mouth and on the forehead. The good news is that people with dry skin usually have fewer blemishes and breakouts caused by trapped oil, unless you are not cleansing at all, in which case you will form the dirt.

**Oily Skin**

Oily skin usually looks shiny, especially in the T-zone areas of the forehead and nose. People with oily skin usually have larger pores, and sometimes, there is a thickening or slightly heavy flaky texture around the nose and chin areas from the accumulation of oil. The bad news is that oily skin is more prone to acne and breakouts. The good news is that oils moisturize the skin so wrinkles are delayed in people with oily skin. In the afternoon, use a tissue on your forehead or on or around the nose area. If you have oily skin, the tissue will pick up the oil.

A concern of mine for oily skin types (and most teenagers) is that they try to use a "sledgehammer to kill a fly." What I am saying is that it is not hard to remove oil from the skin. But, when you buy too strong of a chemical product that strips the skin of all oils, it signals the oil glands to get busy and up the oil production so that the problem becomes even worse. It is important to clean off the excess oil, but there are several gentle, yet effective, ways to do so without stripping the skin.

**Normal Skin**

Normal skin doesn't have extra dryness or a shiny texture. Your skin will have a smooth texture with medium to small pores. The T-zone area may have slightly dry skin and there may be a little more moisture on the forehead and nose area. Breakouts usually are infrequent.

**Sensitive Skin**

Sensitive skin can be dry, but there is an occasional oily or normal skin type that fits this description. Your skin will react to chemicals, weather changes, wind, too much sun, etc. and you may encounter itchy, dry, flaky patches or rashes.

Whatever your age, health or your contact with free radicals, there is a skin regimen for you. The frequently exposed areas of our body, such as our face, throat, hands and sometimes legs and feet, need the most attention. Our face is exposed all the time and it is more fragile than the skin on other areas of our body, so let's start with the facial area.

You do not need a strong cleanser; a gentle cleanser will work for most skin types. Remember, if you have oily skin, over-stripping the skin will cause you more grief then good. For oily to normal skin the gentle Liquid Castile cleanser will work well. Dry, sensitive to normal skin may prefer the cold cream cleanser, which is a slather-on and wipe-off product.

For all skin types, the first step is to remove make-up, then gently cleanse the skin to remove surface dirt and any remaining traces of the make-up remover. Apply your toner. The purpose of the toner is not to just "slap your skin with alcohol." The professional concept is to finish removing any traces of cleanser on the skin and help restore the pH. If your skin is really clean, your body will assist with restoring the pH overnight.

The type of toner you use will depend on your skin type. A stronger toner for oily skin, medium to light toner for normal skin, and a very light toner for dry skin.

Now, your skin is clean and clarified and ready to apply a moisturizer. As you sleep, the moisturizer of your choice will help give you radiant and soft skin, help retard and soften wrinkles and protect your skin pores from dust.

In the morning, you get to skip the make-up removal. (NEVER sleep with make-up on.) Repeat the above process except don't forget to add sunscreen, especially if you live in the sun belt, enjoy winter or summer sports or you live in the "rust belt."

# SKIN CARE

Your skin basically is a water-resistant sack that houses you and renews itself every 27 to 31 days when you are young and may take up to 55 days or so as you age. It often is a reflection of how well you take care of it, both externally and internally. I will not go into detail about good nutrition from the inside, but there are several good books published on the subject matter.

Hormone changes, illness, pollutants, age, etc., will affect the moisture level, fat levels and density of the skin (it thins as we age).

# BASIC CLEANSING ROUTINE

There are four basics you should observe every morning and night for face and neck cleansing and prep.

In the morning: Cleanse, apply toner, moisturize, add sunscreen.

In the evening: Remove make-up, cleanse, apply toner, moisturize.

Cleansing to remove free radicals is essential both morning and night. After a busy day, it's necessary to cleanse your skin from perspiration, contact with your hands on your face, pollutants and UV exposure/UV product. It seems to be self-explanatory, yet, I have been asked, "Why in the morning when all I've done is sleep and I cleansed the night before?"

Keep in mind, your skin renews itself every 30 to 50 days.

During this process, old, dead skin is sloughed off (your body does a good job of this at night). And, let's not forget those little dust mites that love to feast on our dead skin.

Have I grossed you into cleansing in the morning yet? The old skin, if not removed, will fall off. (The amounts are so small at one time you will never see it.) However, it will dull your complexion. By also washing in the morning, you cleanse off old skin and bacteria. If your skin does its job and emits natural sebum (especially if you have oily skin) then dirt in the air sticks to that as well.

I hope I have convinced you about the importance of cleansing. Let's get started making our own natural products, save money and take good care of our skin.

# MAKE-UP REMOVERS

Are you buying expensive make-up remover pads in a jar or bottle? Next time you use up the product, keep the jar, buy those little flat cotton pads they sell for cosmetic use at the dollar store or big-box discount store and make your own. Or, make up four ounces at a time and store in a plastic bottle. Below are two formulas depending on your preference or needs.

## Aloe Non-Greasy Make-up Remover
(non-oily formula)

*This remover will work on all make-ups except waterproof make-up. I state that this is non-oily, but a little added oil creates the extra "glide" to help remove the make-up. In this formula, the aloe vera gel helps make the oil water-soluble, plus it cuts the oil feel so it washes or easily glides off and leaves no oily residue. This formula will work best if you put the mixture in a bottle and apply a small amount to the cotton pad each time you use it.*

**2 ounces (58g) aloe vera gel**
**½ ounce (15ml) safflower oil or mineral oil/baby oil (your choice; I like natural oils better)**

Shelf Life: 1 to 2 months

## Natural and Easy Make-up Remover Pads

*This recipe is great for removing regular and waterproof make-up. Simply soak your little pads in the liquid and stack them in your "replacement" jar. Or, keep this formula in a bottle, your choice.*

1 ounce (30ml) olive oil
1 ounce (30ml) jojoba oil
Optional: 2 to 3 drops of vitamin E oil

Shelf Life: 2 to 3 months

**$ COST COMPARISON**
**Homemade: $3.50 for 2.1 ounces that will moisten many pads**
**Almay™: $5.99 for 65 pads**

# FACIAL CLEANSERS

In the 16th century, Galen invented cold cream. Some current formulas use petroleum or beeswax as the thick emollient. Every ingredient in traditional cold cream has a specific purpose. The wax and oils are used to soften dirt and make-up for easy removal from the skin; water makes it smooth enough to use and the borax binds it together.

## Cold Cream or Cleansing Cream

If you prefer a lighter less oily cleanser, try this formula.

¼ cup (60ml) sweet almond oil
2 tablespoons (29g) melted beeswax
¼ cup (58g) solid white vegetable shortening (the kind that comes in a can)
⅛ teaspoon (.50g) borax
6 tablespoons (90ml) water
½ teaspoon (2.5ml) lemon juice

Pour the wax and oil into a double boiler and stir over low heat until melted together. In a separate pan using low heat, stir the water, lemon juice and borax together until the borax is dissolved. Pour the two heated liquids into the vegetable shortening. Use a mixer or hand beater and beat until cool or it starts to set (get solid). Put in your containers. Add a label with name and make date.

Shelf Life: 2 to 4 months (depends on your climate)

*What could be easier? Buy a nice, but inexpensive, solid vegetable shortening (the kind that comes in a can). Scoop out a little and put it in a pretty jar and use it as a standard cold cream. I had to explain this product to my daughter, Nicole, as cold cream is not promoted too much anymore, although it's available at most grocery stores in the cosmetic section. I think it worked too well and was too inexpensive. The old concept of cold cream was two-fold: an easy way to clean the make-up and grime off your face (place a little on your face and then use a tissue to remove all the make-up, grime and cold cream) and as a moisturizer. After cleansing your face, put on a little more and let it sit for 5 to 10 minutes. Tissue off again for amazingly soft, moisturized skin. To make it fancy, add a drop (go very sparingly) of essential oil. This recipe is best for very dry to normal skin.*

Note: When we go camping in the woods and have limited water, the cold cream is a great product. Put it on and tissue it off. Use the toner of your choice to clarify and then moisturize. Ready for bed — no water needed.

# Homemade Semi-Clear Cold Cream

**¼ cup (57g) aloe vera gel**
**2 tablespoons (30ml) olive or avocado oil (your choice and availability)**

Mix together and store in a container. Label with name and make date.

Shelf Life: 2 weeks

*Remove the grime of pollution and make-up from around your eyes and face area using this recipe. The olive or avocado oil will gently slide the make-up and grime away and leave your skin smooth, but not too oily. The aloe vera gel base helps dissolve the oil and completely remove it from your skin so you are left feeling squeaky clean.*

*Great for both oily and very sensitive skin. You can buy aloe vera gel at a pharmacy, usually with added vitamin E or A. If you have trouble finding it, buy an after-sun cooler that is clear aloe vera gel and use that as the base.*

Note: In my previous career as a formula developer for many companies, I strongly encouraged my customers not to incorporate any kind of fragrance or essential oil to products used around the eyes or the mucus membrane. These areas are easily irritated by fumes from perfumes and/or essential oils. DO THIS AT YOUR OWN RISK.

This facial cleanser which uses liquid Castile soap (found at most health food stores) can be a little smelly, but that can be corrected with a little essential oil. (See note on page 26 regarding fragrance in face products.) I often have been asked where Castile comes from. The first pure olive oil soap (solid and liquid) originated in a town called Castile in Spain. The name stuck for this little simple olive-oil based cleanser...now you know the rest of the story. Liquid Castile soap is a gentle, low-cost base product you can buy to make a multitude of safe and basic home cleansers. Sometimes, you may need to dilute it with water to make it gentler on your face.

This is my top-pick recipe for extra-sensitive to acne-prone to everything skin. This recipe dilutes the liquid Castile for use on the face (even though it is pretty gentle). Add glycerin and aloe vera gel for moisturizing and as a water-soluble ingredient to help slide off the cleanser. Oatmeal milk is optional, but it's great for sensitive skin as a natural skin soother (as is aloe vera gel).

This recipe also uses the liquid Castile and the glycerin adds moisture and glide-off for the cleansing bubbles and grime. For slightly sensitive to normal skin, the witch hazel and rosemary provides extra (yet soft) cleaning power through the natural antibacterial component. The mint (optional) is great for your skin and it helps soften the slightly pungent smell from witch hazel and rosemary.

# Liquid Castile Facial Cleanser
## (for sensitive to normal skin)

2 ounces (60ml) liquid Castile soap (any brand) or make your own, page 50
1 ounce (30ml) water
¼ ounce (8g) glycerin
¼ ounce (8g) aloe vera gel

1 ounce oatmeal milk*
1 cup whole oats (227g)
¾ cup water (180ml)
Cheesecloth

*Oatmeal milk. Gently cook whole oats in ¾ cup (180ml) water for one minute in the microwave. Let sit for one minute. Place the mix into a cheesecloth and squeeze all the liquid from the oatmeal into a bowl using a wringing motion. The liquid you get is called oatmeal milk.

Mix all the ingredients with the oatmeal milk. Store in a plastic or glass bottle. Label with name and make date.

Shelf Life: 2 to 4 months

# Rosemary and Mint Glycerin Cleanser
## (any skin type)

1 ounce (29g) glycerin (vegetable based is best)
2 ounces (60ml) liquid Castile soap
1 ounce (30ml) water
½ ounce (15ml) witch hazel
1 drop rosemary extract
1 drop mint extract

Mix together and store in a plastic or glass bottle. Label with name and make date.

Shelf Life: 3 to 6 months

## USING CLEANSERS

Apply a dime-size amount of cleanser to the palm of your hand or onto a washcloth. Add a small amount of water and start a lather. Then, wash your face and neck gently and avoid pulling on the skin. Use gentle circular motions and avoid the eye area. The skin around the eye area is fine and should be cleansed with eye make-up remover or cold cream and then gently removed. Apply eye cream.

## Aloe, Cucumber and Tea Tree Cleanser
### (normal to oily skin)

*I made this recipe a little stronger. The aloe vera gel and glycerin help with moisture, solubility and glide-off of the cleanser and the other ingredients provide the extra cleaning that oily skin needs (without over-stripping the skin). The cucumber is for clarifying and the tea tree extract is for the antibacterial properties and naturally retarding oil. See more information about Castile soap on page 27.*

3 ounces (90ml) liquid Castile soap (store-bought or homemade, page 50)

1 ounce (29g) aloe vera gel

½ ounce (15ml) water

¼ ounce (7.5ml) glycerin

½ ounce (15ml) witch hazel

1 drop rosemary

1 drop tea tree extract

¼ ounce (7.5ml) cucumber juice*

1 cucumber

3 tablespoons (45ml) water

*Peel ½ cucumber and add three tablespoons (45ml) of water. Puree in the blender and strain. Add the cucumber juice to the other ingredients and mix well. Place in container and label with name and make date.

Shelf Life: 2 to 3 months

**COST COMPARISON**
**Homemade: $1.84 for 5.5 ounces**
**Burt's Bee's™: $7.99 for 4.34 ounces**

## No-Effort Face Cleanser

*Here's how to make the "cheap stuff" better and you will have a high-end cleanser for a much lower price. Note that I am using extracts in small amounts and not fragrance oils.*

1 inexpensive purchased bottle of unscented body cleanser

Water to dilute

Few drops of chamomile extract (for normal or sensitive skin)

Tea tree extract or lemon juice (for oily or problem skin)

Add 10 to 15 percent water to the purchased unscented body cleanser. You will have to remove some of the cleanser from the bottle. Save it for the next batch you make. Then, add a few drops of chamomile extract or lemon juice. Store in bottle and label with name and make date.

Shelf Life: 3 to 6 months

# TONERS

A toner is used after cleansing and before moisturizing. The best way to apply toner is with a cotton ball or cotton cosmetic pad. Apply a small amount of toner to the pad and apply to the face and neck area. (It's better to use an up-sweeping motion than to pull down on your skin.) You also can splash it on with clean fingertips. Avoid the eye area. All these recipes will tone the skin, remove excess cleanser, soothe, clarify and help the skin return to its normal pH.

*Distilled rose water can be purchased at most health food stores. Why distilled water? A trace of toner may stay on your face. There are impurities in a lot of tap water that may leave traces on your skin (see my section on clean water, page 96). It also will help give your product a longer shelf life, as tap water may have residual traces of "other" things. The chamomile extract calms the skin; the witch hazel adds mild toning.*

## Lavender Rose Water Toner
### (sensitive, dry or normal skin)

**½ cup (120ml) rose water or rose water and glycerin**
**¼ cup (60ml) distilled water**
**1 drop lavender essential oil**
**1 tablespoon (15ml) witch hazel**

Blend the ingredients together and keep in a plastic or glass bottle. Label with name and make date.

Shelf Life: Approx. 3 to 4 months

## Alternative Toner

*If you have sensitive skin but want an alternative to the rose water, then use any floral water or lemon juice.*

**½ cup (120ml) distilled water**
**6 drops fresh lemon juice (substitute for rose water)**

Store in bottle with name and make date.

Shelf Life: 1 to 2 months

## Witch Hazel Toner

(for ultra-sensitive skin)

*Here is a very simple toner for ultra-sensitive skin types. Diluted witch hazel with some simple floral water gently helps tone the skin. Most skin that is this sensitive is also very dry, so you don't need much toner. A simple second rinse will make sure all the cleanser is removed before moisturizing.*

½ cup (120ml) distilled water

½ cup (120ml) witch hazel

1 teaspoon (5ml) of brewed chamomile tea (or substitute floral water, lavender or rose)

Blend together and store in a glass or plastic container. Keep in the refrigerator for an extra soothing feel. Label with name and make date.

Shelf Life: 1 to 2 months

## Witch Hazel and Oregano Toner

(for most skin types)

*This toner is an awesome blend for most skin types except extra-sensitive skin (use Witch Hazel Toner recipe above.) The witch hazel is a good, yet gentle, astringent to finish cleaning the skin and the oregano works as an antibacterial (as does tea tree extract).*

½ cup (120ml) witch hazel

¼ cup (60ml) distilled water

2 drops tea tree extract

2 drops oregano oil or extract

Blend together and keep in plastic or glass bottle. Label with name and make date.

Shelf Life: 4 to 6 months

## Rosemary Vodka Toner

(for normal to oily skin)

*Most commercial toners have alcohol as the main ingredient used to "brace and tone" the skin. This recipe works well and it's milder than most commercial brands. The glycerin is used to soften the alcohol and add a bit of moisture back into the toner. This balanced toner is strong enough to curb oily skin without over-stripping the skin.*

½ cup (118ml) distilled water

¼ cup (9ml) plain vodka or Everclear®

⅛ cup (30ml) glycerin

2 drops rosemary extract

Mix all together. Label with name and make date.

Shelf Life: 4 to 5 months

# FACIAL MOISTURIZERS

I often get questioned about the commercial brands on the market and how to judge the quality of the ingredients. At social gatherings, once someone finds out what I did for a living, I can pretty much count on getting asked this question: "So, who has the best product for _____ on the market?"

First, I know products by their ingredients more than their brand names, and second, I really don't like to answer that question without having all the ingredient labels from all the competing companies in front of me and performing some product testing. I cannot answer that "off the cuff."

When writing this book, I knew at some point you would start comparing ingredients and wonder that same thing when looking over skin care products. So I thought I would give you a simple guide to some industry vocabulary and general breakdowns of some good active ingredients that you may encounter. The vocabulary will apply to some of the ingredients in the products you will be making. But, if you want to buy something a little stronger to complement the basics you'll be making at home, I have included some industry active ingredients. You'll find this information in the Glossary.

Now that your skin has been cleansed and prepared, moisturizing would be the last step at night and the second to last step to your morning routine. Sunscreen will be the last morning step if you plan to have any UV (ultraviolet) exposure. We'll discuss sunscreens later. Moisturizers add vital fluid to ease lines and nourish and protect the skin against dryness, but they also help protect the skin from casual free radicals. Most moisturizers can be made at home and the recipes I give you are effective.

## How to Apply

Starting with the neck, place a small amount of moisturizer in your hand and apply using upward strokes. Dot a small amount to the chin, cheeks and forehead, also applying with upward strokes. Apply eye cream around eye area.

I was told that when you couldn't guess a woman's age you should look at her neck and at the back of her hands. These areas usually are cared for the least and can be a better indicator of age. Your lesson? — Make sure when you moisturize that you always apply to your neck and the back of your hands.

The viscosity (refers to the thickness of a product and relates to the amount of oil added for moisturizing purposes) often is the major difference between a lotion and a cream. Knowing this, you can make some good face moisturizers that are a bit thinner (sometimes called a "milk") that will do a great job of moisturizing your face. Sometimes, the density (or viscosity) of commercial creams can be misleading because of unnecessary fillers and thickeners, so viscosity is not always the measurement to quality.

## Daytime Light-Moisture Lotion
### (for oily to normal skin)

This easy-to-make non-greasy lotion works great to moisturize and protect your skin, but not clog your pores. And, you can wear make-up over it without worry. The aloe vera gel is water soluble (used to stretch and extend the oils in water), soothing, will not stimulate sebum production, and it lets your skin breathe, which is really important for all skin but especially oily skin. The beeswax is a natural wax that offers a slight barrier to free radicals. The glycerin is water soluble and a humectant (helps retain moisture as nature's best moisturizer) and just a small amount of a lightweight oil will help protect and soften your skin without being too heavy.

**1 ounce (29g) aloe vera gel**
**1 teaspoon (5ml) melted beeswax**
**2 teaspoons (10ml) glycerin**
**½ teaspoon (2.5ml) avocado oil**

Rapidly stir the ingredients together by hand, then slow down and keep stirring until the beeswax cools, about five to seven minutes. Put in a pretty jar. Label with name and date.

Shelf Life: 2 weeks to 1 month

## Daytime Rich-Moisture Face Cream or Lotion
### (for dry to normal skin)

For dry to normal skin, here is a nice daytime or anytime face moisturizer. Aloe vera gel is added for soothing and the beeswax helps the gel to create a base. Sweet oil is used for lubrication, glycerin and honey for extra moisture and protection, and olive oil for more skin lubrication and soothing.

**1 ounce (29g) aloe vera gel**
**2 tablespoons (30ml) melted beeswax**
**1 teaspoon (5ml) glycerin**
**½ teaspoon (2.5ml) honey**
**3 drops comfrey extract or oil**
**1 teaspoon (5ml) olive oil**

Mix all together. Store in a jar or bottle. Label with name and make date.

Shelf Life: 1 to 2 months

## Night Cream/Lotion

*Using the basics of Daytime Rich-Moisture Face Cream, change the recipe into a night cream by adding the alternate ingredients. The borax is a softener and is fine to use on skin if diluted and in small amounts. It also works to emulsify the lotion. The added moisturizers make the product heavier and more moisturizing for nighttime use. The comfrey introduces natural allantoin, a healing agent that stimulates healthy tissue formation and basic cell proliferation.*

**1 teaspoon (5ml) sweet oil**
**1 teaspoon (5ml) melted cocoa butter**
**½ teaspoon (3g) borax**
**3 tablespoons (45ml) water**
**1 to 2 drops comfrey extract or oil**
**1 to 2 drops vitamin E oil**

Boil water and add borax. Stir until borax is dissolved. Mix the borax solution with the other ingredients and store in a jar or similar container. Label with name and make date.

Shelf Life: 1 to 2 months

*For a special skin treatment, dampen comfrey tea bags and apply (cooled) right to your face to gain skin-strengthening compounds.*

## Moisturizing Facial Treatment

**2 teaspoons (10ml) sweet oil**
**2 drops vitamin E oil**

Mix together. Store in a container labeled with name and make date.

Shelf Life: 2 to 3 months

*This is a deep therapy treat for your skin.*

*Apply the oil like a face cream to your face and neck. Put leftovers on the back of your hands. Leave on for 30 minutes, then gently cleanse, tone and moisturize your skin.*

## Cheap and Simple Moisturizer

**Mayonnaise or vegetable shortening**

Make as much as you want. Apply to your face and neck. Use immediately.

*In a pinch, this moisturizer works great.*

# EYE CREAMS

*Because the skin around the eyes is thinner than almost anywhere else on your body, this area needs special care. We all want to minimize wrinkles and lines so moisture in this area is really helpful. However, if you use a cream that is too heavy for this area, it can actually add to the puffiness around your eyes.*

*Here are two light, but effective, eye creams you can make yourself. Since everyone's skin is thinner and more delicate around the eye area and there are not many oil glands located in this area, eye creams can be used by any skin type.*

## Light Comfrey and Aloe Eye Cream
(for any skin type)

**¼ cup (59g) aloe vera gel**
**4 drops comfrey extract (or make concentrate from tea bag)**
**½ teaspoon (2.5ml) cucumber juice***
**1 cucumber**
**3 tablespoons (45ml) water**

*Peel ½ cucumber and add three tablespoons (45ml) of water. Puree in the blender and strain. Add the cucumber juice to the other ingredients. Mix together and apply to the eye area. Store in a jar labeled with name and make date.

Shelf Life: Up to 3 weeks — Keep in the refrigerator.

## Antioxidant Moisturizing Night Eye Cream With Vitamin E
(for any skin type)

**¼ cup (59g) aloe vera gel**
**One 500 IU vitamin E oil-based capsule**
**2 to 3 drops green tea extract (or make concentrate from tea bag)**

Pierce the capsule and squeeze the contents into the aloe vera gel. Mix together and apply. Store in jar labeled with name and make date.

Shelf Life: Up to 3 weeks — Keep in the refrigerator.

**COST COMPARISON**
**Homemade: $1.02 for 2 ounces**
**Este Lauder™: $48.00 for 2 ounces**
**Burt's Bees: $24.99 for 2 ounces**

# FOR THE GUYS IN YOUR LIFE

I have a husband, a son and three older brothers, so I am sensitive about leaving the men out of this information. In the old days, men would just about go into crisis if you suggested they moisturize, tone, spa or do anything much more than splash on an aftershave. Today, most men have realized that if they don't want to look like a piece of old leather as they get older (and of course we are all living much longer thanks to medical science and changing lifestyle habits), they also must do some basic skin care and protect their skin from the sun. Whole skin-care lines and men's spas have become commonplace as old traditions blur. Men, as a whole, have thicker skin but they still break down into the same skin types as women: sensitive, dry, normal (some T-zone oil) and oily. Men actually can use some of the same skin care products as women. Below is an aftershave toner for men that is appropriate for all skin types except super sensitive. Substitute the super-sensitive face toner on page 31 for an aftershave. You also may want to "customize" men's products with either a few drops of their (or your) favorite cologne, essential oil blend, or a few drops of rum or citrus extract to make a scent that is more favorable to them (and you).

## Aftershave Splash Toner for Men

*Instead of buying that expensive aftershave that is primarily alcohol, make your own. It also makes a great gift. The alcohol or witch hazel provides the toning, the chamomile calms the area and the sage/mint/rosemary helps clarify and buffer the skin so that the skin can restore to its proper pH. For guys with sensitive skin, use witch hazel instead of the vodka.*

¼ cup (59ml) vodka or Everclear

3 to 4 drops chamomile extract or essential oil

1 teaspoon (5ml) sage tea* (can substitute mint or rosemary)

A few drops men's cologne, rum or citrus extract (or an essential oil )

*You also can make the sage tea by steeping sage leaves, if desired. Add the cologne, extract or oil to your preference. Store in a nice bottle. Label with name and make date.

Shelf Life: 4 to 6 months

## Quick and Super-Simple Toner

*In an emergency, you can use 50 percent diluted vinegar, vodka or Everclear as a toner. A little stronger for oily skin, diluted for more sensitive skin. Tea also makes a great emergency toner for your skin. Green tea will nourish and provide free-radical help, especially in heavily polluted areas and after sun exposure. Chamomile, lavender and rose will calm the skin and is best used on sensitive skin. Mint, sage or rosemary revitalize the skin with slight astringent properties and is best for normal to oily skin.*

Vinegar, vodka or Everclear diluted 50 percent with water

A variety of teas including green, chamomile, rosemary, mint, sage, lavender or rose

Apply to face and neck with hands or cotton pads. Use immediately.

# SUNSCREENS, UVA AND UVB EXPOSURE

Sun protection is one of the easiest beauty secrets we have to avoid premature aging and keeping our skin young, moist and healthy. Wear sunscreen. Wear a hat. Protect your eyes. Wear new SPF (Sun Protection Factor) clothing.

Zinc oxide and titanium dioxide help deflect the sun, but leave you a little pale. The problem is, I have no way of rating the effectiveness of sunscreens, so I would not know how much to have you apply. As sunscreens are a pharmaceutically rated product, I am going to suggest that you buy this product. I will, however, cover information about the kinds of damaging ultraviolet rays and ways to protect yourself.

There are three kinds of ultraviolet rays:

Ultraviolet A (UVA)

Ultraviolet B (UVB)

Ultraviolet C (UVC)

UVA and UVB are the only rays that currently penetrate the

ozone layer of the earth, so we will concern ourselves with the A and B rays.

When UVA and UVB rays land on your skin, the melanocyte cells (melanin at work) in the basal layer of your skin go to work. Your ethnic background determines how much melanin you have in your skin. The more of a European or fair skin type you have, the more susceptible you are to burns, cancer, early wrinkles and discolored skin spots from the sun's damaging rays. If you have darker skin, you may have a little more natural protection, but you are still a target of cancer and skin damage. UVA rays are greater in number but less intense. UVB rays are shorter in number but more intense and more dangerous.

**Sunscreen Q & A**

What if you're in the water? Both types of rays can penetrate water up to three feet, so don't think because your body is in the water that you are not getting sun exposure. If the sun is shining on the water, you also are absorbing the rays. Even on cloudy days 65 to 80 percent of UVA/UVB rays will make it through to your skin.

By the pool in the shade? Ever heard of UVA/UVB bounce? Yes, that's right; when the UVA/UVB rays come down and hit anything remotely shiny like water, a light-colored wall, even grass to a lesser degree, the rays will "bounce" (at a lesser strength) and possibly head right for you.

Is it a little windy? Yes, you guessed it, UVA/UVB rays in the atmosphere can be carried right in the wind. Did you ever hear of wind burn?

Indoors and in the car? Aside from the rays hitting you directly through the glass, they can "bounce" off water or other substances as mentioned above and come through the glass (to a lesser degree). But hey, we are talking accumulated damages here. UVA and UVB damage accumulates. You need to wear sunscreen during the day, especially if you are going to be outside, it's summer, snow is on the ground (a lot of bounce off all that white) or if you live in the sun belt. Protect yourself to stay young looking.

Moisture oils and the sun are not always a good mix. Remember, anything resembling oils and glosses that you put on your body (this includes the lips) will work like frying oil depending on the amount of oil used. Don't be afraid to moisturize, and use SPF lip balm with sunscreen on top to compensate.

Always remember this my dear reader. In my profession as a skin care formulator for many years, sun-worshiping divas begged me to make a lot of anti-aging skin care products to counteract some of the damage they had bestowed on their skin from years of sun worship. For me, it was job security, but for you, follow my motto: "an ounce of prevention is worth way more than a gallon of an anti-aging cream cure or a visit to the plastic surgeon."

There are between 50 to 60 sunscreen agents at my last count. The best and most important product will have on its label, "BROAD SPECTRUM UVA/UVB PROTECTION." Sunscreens can cause reactions. If you have sensitive skin, always test a small amount on the inside of your arm, halfway between your wrist and elbow. Wait 12 to 24 hours to make sure it is a good product for you. Also, get the full-spectrum product labeled for "Babies and Children" as they are designed to be gentler. Then, use this product often. There are specialty sunscreens designed for the face with gentler ingredients, but make sure that it has full-spectrum protection.

Avoiding the sun in the most intense part of the day is pretty much common knowledge (between the hours of 10:00 a.m. and 2:00 p.m.) but sometimes that is not possible, and you still may be subject to "bounce." Aside from staying indoors during the day (we do have lives to live) sunscreens with the full coverage SPF become our next best option.

The number on the bottle of sunscreen lists an SPF (Sun Protection Factor) number which gives you an indication of how long you can stay in the sun without suffering the effects of UVB's burning rays (currently, only UVBs are rated). This is not a perfect science because there are so many skin colors and types. This is how the ratings work. Based on your knowledge of how long you can stay in the sun without burning is how you gauge which SPF will work for you. For example, you are fair and can only be in the direct sun 15 minutes without burning. If you use a product that is an SPF 10, it means that you can stay in the sun 10 times longer without getting burned. If you can tolerate 15 minutes, your personal unprotected burn tolerance times 10 SPF = 150 minutes, which is 2.5 hours. Then, you must realize that an SPF 10 only blocks out about 90 percent (give or take a little) of the sun's harmful rays. You also must allow for the strength of the conditions: you are on the water (lots of bounce and full rays); you're at a high altitude (closer to the sun means more intense rays); it's 12:00 p.m. and the sun is straight up in the sky. All these factors play a roll in how effective your coverage will be. There is also the fact that you can swim off or sweat off your sunscreen in hot weather. It is all pretty complicated. To make it easy for you, and so you don't have to make calculations every time you go outside, I'm providing some simple recommendations.

- Buy full-spectrum sunscreen.

- I recommend at least an SPF of 15 if you have tan or darker skin and SPF 30 to 45 if you are very fair. Apply two coats of sunscreen. Apply once, let dry, then apply again. Why? There was another factor we did not talk about — thickness of coverage. Most manufacturers do not tell you what the thickness of coverage is for the recommended rating. If you apply it too thinly, your SPF 30 may only give you an SPF 15. By letting it dry and reapplying, you have a good shot of getting the right coverage as rated.

- Figure out how long you think you can stay in the sun without protection, then do the math as given above. Be sure to reapply your sunscreen at that time if you are still in the sun.

- If you swim or sweat a lot, reapply your sunscreen more often.

- The average shelf life of ingredients in a sunscreen product is about a year. Do not use old sunscreen products (older than a year), they may not give you the protection you need.

- The very best way to treat damaged skin — prevent it.

# BODY MOISTURIZERS

Deep treat extra-dry areas like your elbows, knees and heels by making and using these wonderful body moisturizers. Before applying, use an exfoliating tool or an exfoliation scrub. See Home Spa Treatments, page 55. Then, use pure cocoa butter or coconut oil to soften. See page 73 for the moisturizing paraffin treatment.

### HELP FOR VERY DRY HANDS AND FEET

Get an old pair of light mittens (they may get a little oily) and use as a sleeve at night for moisturizing your hands. Slather hands with body butter or a mix of 50/50 melted cocoa butter and olive oil and put your hands in baggies (or wrap in plastic wrap). Use rubber bands if needed, but not too tight, you don't want to cut off your circulation. Place hands in the mittens. For your feet, use old socks after wrapping in plastic wrap. Go to bed and in the morning you will find soft beautiful skin.

In-a-pinch moisturizer — use vegetable shortening, olive oil or mayonnaise. In-a-pinch body butter shortcut — straight cocoa butter or straight shea butter.

## The Great Basic Creamy Body Lotion

*Here is a great body lotion recipe. The combination of beeswax and oils with aloe will moisturize without being too heavy. It is great for all skin types — even sensitive skin. If you have very sensitive skin, you may want to leave out the fragrance unless you have one that you know works for you.*

¼ cup (59g) aloe vera gel
⅛ cup (30g) beeswax
½ cup (118ml) apricot kernel oil, sweet almond oil or olive oil (your choice)
8 drops jojoba oil
3 teaspoons (15ml) borax

Melt the oil of choice, the jojoba oil and the beeswax together in a small pan on low setting. In a separate bowl, mix the aloe vera gel and borax together until the borax is dissolved. When the beeswax-oil solution is melted and stirred, remove from the heat and then slowly add it to the aloe-borax mixture. Keep stirring for about five minutes. Add fragrance or essential oil if desired and stir for about another minute. If the mixture is too thin and you would like it thicker, reheat the mixture on low and add more melted beeswax. Remove from the heat and stir for one minute. If you want it thinner, warm and add more oil. Put in cute little tubs or bottles. Label with name and make date.

Note: Heat will disperse fragrance, so if you reheat it, you may want to add more fragrance or essential oil as it is cooling.

Shelf Life: 1 to 2 months — Keep in the refrigerator.

## The Better Body Butter

*Body butters are a treat anytime and best for normal to dry skin. Butters are especially good after exposure to wind, cold and chafing and after too much sun or salt exposure. The oils will slather your skin and leave you feeling moisturized and pampered. This recipe uses cocoa butter, shea butter and natural oils. If you cannot find shea butter, make it with the cocoa butter.*

2 tablespoons (30g) aloe vera gel
¼ cup (59g) cocoa butter or a blend of 50/50 shea butter and cocoa butter to equal this amount
2 teaspoons (10ml) grape seed oil
1 teaspoon (5ml) safflower oil

Melt the oils together on very low heat. Remove from the heat and stir in the aloe vera gel.
Optional: Add a few drops (two to three) essential oil, fragrance oil or extract, if desired. If you live in a cold climate, occasionally you may need to warm the butter to soften it. Store in a container labeled with name and make date.

Shelf Life: 3 to 6 months

# BODY WASHES

## EXTEND YOUR BODY WASH

Do you have an expensive body wash that you just love but it sets back your pocketbook? Reduce the cost of that item by adding an extender. Stir one teaspoon (5g) of pectin into one cup (240ml) of hot water (or follow instructions on pectin box for thickening water) then add that solution into your favorite body wash for a 75 percent body wash to 25 percent solution. You just saved 25 percent on the cost of that product! This will work on most products. Try a small amount first to test compatibility.

## Gentle Moisturizing Body Wash

**2 cups (473ml) liquid Castile soap**
**1 tablespoon (15ml) glycerin**
**3 to 4 drops essential oil**

Mix and use as needed. Store in a bottle labeled with name and make date.

Shelf Life: 4 to 6 months

## Rosemary Almond Toning Body Wash

**2 cups (473ml) liquid Castile soap**
**1 teaspoon (5ml) witch hazel**
**4 drops rosemary essential oil**
**¼ teaspoon (1.25ml) almond extract**

Mix and use. Store in container labeled with name and make date.

Shelf Life: 4 to 6 months

# DEODORANTS

My mother used to say, "men sweat, women glisten." Well, a fun thought, but however you want to paint it — sweat happens. It is one of the ways our body gets rid of impurities and adjusts our body temperature. Eccrine and apocrine glands (there are many and they are distributed in different areas of the body) respond to overheating, physical exertion, stress and hormone changes. As we age, they become a little less active because the aging skin cells contract to partially close off sweat ducts and we perspire up to 30 percent less. There has to be some advantages to getting older! Secreted fluids (decomposing fluids from the body mixed with bacteria) are what makes our perspiration smell. Making it worse are things we consume such as caffeine, garlic and other foods.

OK, now we have some background...what to do about the smell until we can wash it off?

## Homemade Deodorant

*The aloe vera gel is used as a natural base to hold the formula together. The baking soda is a natural absorbent and deodorant. The chlorophyll helps destroy odor-forming bacteria. Chlorophyll may be hard to find in liquid form so you may need to buy it in a gel capsule and then pierce it to squeeze out the liquid.*

¼ cup (59g) aloe vera gel
1 tablespoon (15g) baking soda
15 drops chlorophyll

Mix together and apply small amounts to armpits just as you would regular deodorant. Store in a container labeled with name and make date.

Shelf Life: Up to 1 month

## Deodorant Dusting Powder

*In some areas of Asia where they have no air conditioning, they dust this on their sheets at night with a small shaker can to keep them cool and to absorb any nighttime perspiration. I tried it and it was lovely. They only use fine rice powder.*

¼ cup (62g) baking soda
½ cup (124g) cornstarch, arrowroot powder or rice powder (I prefer fine rice powder)

Mix together. Apply to clean dry armpits. You can add it to shoes as a foot deodorant with mild antiperspirant action. Store in a shaker container labeled with name and make date.

Shelf Life: 12 months

## QUICK AND EASY PERSPIRATION SOLUTION

According to research, consuming 50mg of zinc daily can greatly reduce the amount of perspiration you give off. Drinking six to eight ounces of water a day will reduce how pungent your perspiration is, therefore reducing the strength of the odor.

# SOAPS

## Basic Instructions and Troubleshooting
## Read This First!

Here is some information about what can go wrong with melt-and-pour techniques:

- When you are adding fragrance (with essential oils, of course), try not to add more than one percent of the essential oil to the soap. In simple terms, do not add more than about three or four drops per four-ounce soap bar that you are melting. If you over-fragrance, you can upset the balance of the soap and it will not reset properly. Remember, a little goes a long way with essential oils. When choosing a fragrance to use, make sure it is a good quality essential oil. Do not use perfume or cologne because it is too diluted and will not give you enough fragrance for the amount you need and to use more would just overload the soap.

- Do not bring the soap to a boil in any form; keep the burner on low even if it takes longer to melt. Even a few bubbles can ruin the soap (it gathers too much moisture when it sets up). People sometimes ask me if they can use the microwave for this process. The answer is yes, but again, do not boil. Be prepared to ruin a couple of batches until you get your microwave's temperatures figured out — the boiling point happens very fast in a microwave!

- Do not be tempted to put your newly poured soap in the refrigerator to setup; the soap will gather moisture and later it will look like it's crying. Just let the soap setup in a cool, dry place overnight. If it's very humid, let it setup in an air-conditioned room, away from the air conditioner; otherwise, room temperature is fine.

- Do not add essential oil when the soap is at its hottest. Let the melted mixture sit for three to five minutes while you stir, then add the essential fragrance and color. Essential oils are like vitamins: they lose some of their effectiveness in high heat. Many professional soap makers have called me with problems about their fragrance not "holding." Most of the time, the problem was they "cooked" the fragrance right out of their batch when they were making the soap. Technique is everything in this craft!

- You can use store-bought food colorings to color your soaps, but be advised that although the colorings are safe to use, they are water soluble and will color your skin. It may take a day or two to come off or fade if the coloring was full strength. The bottom line? Keep your soap colors pastel. The question I frequently get asked is: "How much color do I use?" While it seems like a logical question, and indeed I can give exact answers for everything else, my answer probably leaves the person feeling a little silly. What shade do you want it, what is the volume size, and how dark do you want it? Color is subjective. In other words, you just have to play with this. Yes, you can mix colors together like paint colors (red and blue make purple, yellow and red make orange, blue and yellow make green, and so on), but be creative! My main warning for using color — go easy on the quantity and stay with pastels. Even though this color is safe, no one wants to use a midnight blue soap and then try to wash a second time to get the color off his or her hands. Again, a little goes a long way with colors. For a four-ounce soap bar, one drop of food coloring will give you a medium shade.

- Only use plastic and rubber molds. For molded soaps, you can use those cute plastic candy molds you find at craft and cake-decorating stores. Plastic "flexes" and allows you to easily unmold after the soap is setup. Do not use metal, and especially don't use plaster molds because the soap soaks right into the plaster and tries to moisturize it! Milk cartons that are waxed and can be torn away from the mold also are fine to use. You will know your soap is setup when it is dry and pops out with just a little encouragement (twisting). The bigger the soap mold, the longer the setup time. When you unmold your creation, air dry for just a few hours, then wrap in plastic until ready to use (glycerin loves to pull moisture from the air to your skin; if there is no skin, it will accumulate moisture from the air). If it is going to be a gift, put it in a plastic bag, tie the top with a ribbon and store in a cool, dry place (soaps have a very long shelf life).

Now that you understand the basic dos and don'ts, it's time to play!

I am giving you one basic soap recipe, as there are several good books published which specialize in all varieties of soap making. There is enough information here for you to understand the process. Since I have used liquid Castile as an ingredient quite often in the book, I thought it only appropriate that I give you a formula for an olive oil (Castile type) soap and then tell you how to dilute it into your own liquid Castile soap. In the back of the book you will find sources for other books on soap making, as it is a whole topic in itself.

*This wonderful soap will be slightly amber in color, very mild and lather well. And best of all, you can use the solid for remelting projects, or convert this into liquid soap for use in other recipes in the book. You will need a simple kitchen scale that measures ounces.*

*Caution: You will be working with lye which is an acid that can and will burn you. When handling this part of the process, use gloves, apron, safety glasses and protect counters and surfaces from this ingredient. Lye is necessary in soap manufacturing, but when it is cooked during the process, the acid changes to alkaline and becomes very safe. It is the lye that renders the fat (olive oil) and through cooking turns it into a solid and congeals it.*

*This process requires care and it is not safe for children to participate until saponification is done.*

## Basic Olive Oil Soap

**50 ounces (1L) olive oil (the better the quality of oil, the better your soap)**
**2 ounces (59ml) coconut oil**
**7 ounces (218g) lye**
**19 ounces (562ml) cold water**

**Supplies**
**2 large double boilers (some people use a large pots, but a double boiler gives me more temperature control)**
**4 measuring containers**
**Kitchen scale**
**Stove top burner**
**2 cooking thermometers**
**Wooden spoon**
**Gloves**
**Apron**
**Safety glasses**
**A large plastic pan for cut soaps or plastic soap molds (can use decorative candy molds)**
**Safety equipment a must!**

Always pre-measure your empty containers then deduct the weight of the container so that whatever ingredient is in the container is the correct weight.

## SAFETY EQUIPMENT

Before you begin, put on long rubber gloves, an apron and goggles. Do not put the lye out or make up a lye solution and then leave unattended. The hardest part of making this soap (or in most soap making for that matter) is getting the temperatures the same in the lye solution and the oil mix when you add them together.* Most likely if your soap doesn't turn out — it was here where the problem started.

### Soap Instructions

- Note: Use a separate container for each ingredient. Weigh out the correct amount of lye and place in a glass container. Set aside, keeping it away from heat and other ingredients.

- Repeat for the olive oil, coconut oil and water. (Do not mix – all need to stay in separate containers.)

- Make sure you and your surfaces are protected. Add the lye to the double boiler or large pot. Be careful not to splash the lye (you would be splashing acid). Slowly pour the water into the lye, NOT the lye into the water.

- Slowly stir the water and lye mix with a WOODEN spoon until the lye is dissolved. This mixture will self-heat and heat upwards to 190°F (88°C). Remove from heat. Let it cool down to about 120°F (49°C). You are getting ready for the hardest part of soap making.*

- Heat the olive oil and coconut oil together in a double boiler on low. Using a thermometer, get the temperature to 100-105°F (38-39°C).

- The trick is to watch the temperature in the lye solution while not overheating the oil solution so that both solutions are between 95-105°F (26-38°C). When the oil mix and the lye mix are at the same temperature, around 100°F (38°C), add the lye solution very slowly into the oil mixture, stirring constantly. It should be a thin steady stream. (I prefer to have someone help me, as sometimes it's hard to do this yourself.) Make sure your helper follows all the safety rules for working with lye.

The constant stirring will make sure the lye is absorbed evenly into the oil (fats).

- After everything is mixed together, keep stirring. It is important to keep the blend forming. Now the labor begins. Turn off the heat, but leave the pot on the burner and keep stirring. Slowly, the mix will start to thicken and get a cloudy (opaque) appearance and then become slightly grainy looking. The length of time depends on the temperature and moisture levels in the air where you live. A short time would be 15 to 20 minutes and a long time would be 30 to 45 minutes.

- You want the mixture to become thick enough that if you swirl your spoon in the top of the mix, it leaves a little design. (It will be a very slight design in this mix. If you have stirred 40 minutes and don't see the design, you are done anyway.)

- Pour the mixture into your molds. If you are not using molds and want to make bars, pour the soap mixture into a large plastic pan.

- When the soap mixture is completely hardened, pop out the whole soap block. Use pressure on the sides and the back of the pan to loosen first. Then, use a hot knife, or better yet, a hot wire, to score and cut your bars to your desired size.

- This soap is very moisturizing, so you may find a small amount of oil that rises to the top when cool. Use a paper towel and wipe the bars down. To store, wrap in plastic wrap.

*If you buy commercial Castile bar soaps, you can follow this recipe as well to make your own liquid Castile. You also can purchase liquid Castile at most health food stores.*

## RECYCLING SOAP SCRAPS

How many times have you used a soap bar, got it down to a small size and thought, it's too hard to hold onto and use or it's not worth saving. Most people throw those bits of soap away, but wait! Start a small collection in an old, washed, cottage cheese container or pickle jar. At year-end, you can make pretty guest soaps or gift items.

Some stores carry soap flakes which are basic shavings from old-fashioned soaps. The flakes also can be used in these recipes.

## WASTE NOT; WANT NOT — RECYCLED "FIREWORKS" SOAP

Chop up all your soap scraps into small sizes, then heat a soap base. You can use a white opaque or clear soap base depending on the look you want. As the base starts to cool and form a slight film while setting up, place chunks of soap scraps into the pot and swirl around. Immediately, pour into molds and you will have little "fireworks" or color chunks in the soap. Good clean recycling!

# Making Liquid Castile Soap

8 ounces (224g) of your homemade bar soap, or Castile bar soap
32 ounces (946ml) warm water
¾ ounces (23g) powdered pectin (the type used for making jams and jellies)

Remelt the bar soap using low heat. Add the warm water and pectin. Stir until cool. Pour into bottles and label with name and make date.

Shelf Life: 3 to 4 months

# Recycled Soap Balls

**Soap base or melted scraps**
**Vegetable shortening**
**Spoon**
**Wax paper**
**Optional: Ice cream scoop**

Apply vegetable shortening to your hands or an ice cream scoop so the soap doesn't stick. After the melted soap begins to cool and becomes somewhat firm, but not completely hard, scoop out portions with a spoon. Shape into balls and place on wax paper to finish hardening. The nice thing about soap is that if you don't find the right consistency the first time, you can remelt it and try again. Wrap in plastic and store in appropriate location. Label with name and make date.

Shelf Life: 12 months

## Old-Fashioned Shaving Soap

*A good shaving soap is soft, and when you dampen the brush and swirl a couple of times in the soap container, it is ready to use. The consistency should be halfway between a hard solid and liquid. Solid enough to hold its shape as a firm mush, but not hard like a soap.*

**Homemade or purchased soap base**
**Water to equal half the soap**

Melt the soap base. Add the water and stir until mushy. Store in a cute co[ntainer] with a shaving brush. Label with name and make date.

Shelf Life: 4 to 6 months

## Soap On a Rope

*Wow! This is easy. Melt the soap, pour into a mold or shape into round balls. (See Recycled Soap Balls page 50.)*

After soap is made, create two holes for the placement of the rope. Insert the long end of a spoon (or something else of you choice) through the top section of the soap and twirl in a circle to make the holes for the rope or fancy cord. Attach your desired length of cord/rope and then pour more warm soap into the hole with cord/rope facing up. Wait for it to harden. Make sure you put a hole deep enough into the soap so it stays connected through the life of the soap.

## Basic Soap Molding

*You can make these soaps at a fraction of the cost of purchased soap. This is a simple melt-and-pour method.*

**You can use clear glycerin soap or opaque (white soap) for this method**
**Color and essential oil, if desired**
***Molds of your choice**

Melt the soap base slowly on low heat. Once it is melted, remove from heat (this is where you add the color and fragrance after a short cool-down, if you wish). Next, simply pour the soap into your molds. Let setup overnight or until the soap easily pops out of the mold.
Wrap in plastic, or take straight to your bathroom for use. Wasn't that easy? Label with name and make date.

# Oatmeal and Lavender Soap

**Clear glycerin soap or opaque (white soap) for this method**
**Lavender flowers**
**Oatmeal, grated**

Method 1 (not shown): Melt the soap base slowly on low heat. Add lavender flowers and stir into the soap. Pour the soap into a pan. When the soap is starting to setup, stir in grated oatmeal. Usually, the oatmeal will "float" throughout the soap, which will give you a layered look.

Method 2 (shown below): Melt the soap base slowly on low heat. Put the lavender flowers and oatmeal in the bottom of the pan. Pour the soap over the lavender flowers and oatmeal. Wrap in plastic wrap and label with name and make date.

## Toy or Decal in Soap

**Clear glycerin soap**
**Essential oil, if desired**
**Rubber or plastic toys of your choice (these must fit into the soap mold and be no**
**more than half the size of the mold)**
**Or, coated two-sided decal**

Melt the soap base slowly on low heat. Remove when melted. If desired, add fragrance.

You do not want to just set the item in the bottom of the mold because when you unmold, it won't be suspended in the soap (it sadly will be sitting on the bottom). To suspend items in soap, you must first create a soap "stand" for the item within the soap. This means that you will be pouring only a portion of your soap base into the mold, then later remelting the balance of soap and pouring into the mold.

If you are putting in a toy, decide by the size of the toy where you want it (height-wise) in the soap. Pour the first layer of soap just a little under that height.

If you are putting in a decal, pour the soap to fill half of the mold.

Let the first layer of soap setup until it is almost firm with just a slight bit of moisture on top and it easily holds the toy or decal in the middle. If you leave it until it is totally setup and dry on top, the two layers of soap will not stick together. You want the first layer of soap to be firm enough to hold and not "break through" when you pour the final layer. (I wish I could give you an exact time, but it depends on the size of the mold.)

Now, remelt the base again on low heat, set the toy or decal in place, and slowly spoon the melted soap over the item until enough depth is achieved that you can gently pour the rest of the soap to the top. With any luck, you will only have to do two stages, not three, unless that's what you desire.

*This recipe works better with no added color, but if you want color, use a very, very pastel color or you won't see the toy or decal inside. A lovely Cameo decal in soap makes a charming gift for grandma. Do you know someone who collects animals? Give him or her a darling animal soap — like the frog shown here — for the bathroom. A mom will thank you when you give soap with a toy in it — what will her child have to do to get the toy? Wash, of course. Maybe we can trick little Johnny into that bath after all.*

*Want rainbow or two-color soap? Follow the same layering process described here but don't put anything in it; just color each layer a different color. You can use essential oils to make each layer a different, but synergistic, therapy smell...Are you feeling creative yet?*

*...oy, are ... all of ... s and ...ooking soaps made? Here's how — and you don't even need to be a pro to do this at home. Again, it is simply technique when you use both clear glycerin soap and white (opaque) soap.*

*Using this recipe, we will suspend opaque soap chunks in clear soap. Once you get the hang of this, you will want to try making it many different ways to see the patterns like those shown in the samples.*

## Soap by the Slice

**1 to 2 pounds (448g to 896g) clear glycerin soap**
**8 to 12 ounces (23g to 34g) white (opaque or non-clear) soap**
**Color**
**Essential oils**

Divide the white soap into three equal portions. Melt each portion separately. Take the first white portion, melt over low heat on the stove top, color it (your choice), and pour it into a plastic square or rectangular container.

After it sets up, unmold and use the knife to cut into uneven chunks. Repeat this process with the other two portions of white soap, coloring each a different color. Set them aside until needed.

Take the full amount of clear glycerin and melt over low heat. Meanwhile, arrange a few (⅛ to ½) assorted colors of soap chunks at random in the bottom of a plastic loaf pan. When the clear glycerin is melted, you have a decision to make. You will be pouring this into the pan around the white chunks. If you pour the glycerin soap while it is very hot, it will make more of a solid chunk with a marbled effect because some of the chunks will melt (if not all). If you want to clearly see the chunks, let the glycerin base cool for 15 to 20 minutes before pouring or spooning into the pan. Pour just enough to cover the tops of the chunks. If you like this height, you can stop here, but usually it is too short. Either way, you must wait for this layer to setup until firm and slightly moist on top if you are going to layer again; otherwise, see the next section.

Repeat the whole process one or two more times until you get the "height" you want for your soap block.

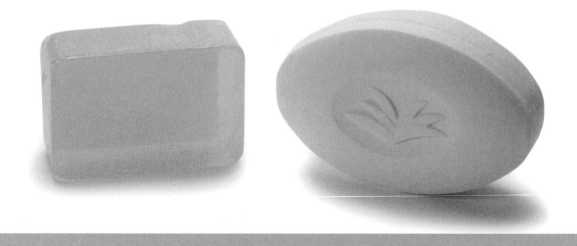

When totally setup (this is a lot of soap and setup may take one to three days depending on depth) take the soap out of the pan.

Now it's time to cut the slices (this is not for children). With the knife, score (do not cut) lines for how thick you want the soap slices. Make small marks along the side of the bar (like cutting a bread loaf). With glycerin soap, if you try to cut it with a knife, it will splinter. (We didn't care if the soap chunks were perfect.) We want beautiful perfect slices, so turn a stove burner on medium-high and put on heavy electrical or work gloves. Take a thin- to-medium-gauge metal wire, long enough to stretch across the burner and wrap around your gloved hands at least once, ensuring a sure grip. Briefly hold the wire over the burner after it is on full heat (mind your gloved hands). It will take about 5 to 10 seconds for the wire to get very hot. Metal conducts heat very well, which is why you need adequate protection for your hands while holding the wire. Using the marks where you have scored the soap, quickly slice the soap using the whole width of the hot wire. It will cut beautifully and you will get to see the treasures inside that were made during the pouring process.

Now that you understand this concept, you do not have to only make chunks of soap. You can use molds to create shapes, suspend items in your soap or try putting strips of a colored opaque or transparent soap in another colored opaque base. Play with different looks and shapes and have fun!

# HOME SPA TREATMENTS

Now, it's time to relax and pamper yourself. When speaking with so many of my clients, there seems to be guilt associated with the word SPA. It's as if it's not necessary or we don't deserve to be treated to such luxury. And sometimes, we have a "thing" about putting ourselves last...so this is how it works. You must read this SPA introduction!

You always have to help others before helping yourself. Is that what just flashed in your mind? Read on....We often put ourselves last, something to do with being selfish, feeling guilty, etc. Well, I am giving you permission to toss that notion out right now. If we are going to affect change, one of the longest journeys we may need to take is the one between our two ears.

I want to start with the "feel good" things you can do for yourself to feel motivated, pampered, cared for, and most importantly — feel good about yourself. First, we'll look at doing some simple and fun things to bring our costs way down. Remember, thinking economically is not "being cheap;" rather it's being "economically sound." And, it's OK if you save enough money to take a nice vacation or put more toward the college fund.

So, when you scan the chapters and you're tempted to jump to making the other stuff first and once again put yourself last, remember, you will do a better job and feel better about making the other recipes if you do something for yourself first.

I offer you some wisdom from Dr. Dyer, who once spoke about the overall issues of putting yourself last, feeling guilt, etc.

You cannot help something or someone to wellness if you yourself are ill.

You cannot help others out of poverty if you yourself are poor.

You cannot feed others if you yourself are hungry.

Need I go on? This is where I start to get you feeling good about saving money, making easier and safer products and being more environmentally friendly. It can be fun and stock your shelves! First, make and enjoy a few of these recipes for yourself and savor the experience. Then, take a look at all the other recipes and tips I give you to save money and make your life simpler and healthier.

## SPA IDEAS

- Sponsor a "spa night" with your friends. Pick out a recipe for each person, have them make it and bring extra to share. It would be like a cookie exchange but a spa product exchange instead.

- Have a party where everyone takes turns giving each other treatments with lots of laughs and girl chatter for a relaxing fun evening and a chance to try all the recipes. Each person makes one recipe; then choose your favorite.

- Get together with friends and have each person make enough of one specific recipe (packaged in individual containers) for everyone invited. Exchange products with everyone. You'll go home with lots of goodies and you didn't have to spend a lot of money. Find out from your friends which product they liked best or what was the easiest to make. Saves you time and money!

# MASSAGE

Aaahhhh! Nothing is nicer than this simple getaway. I will say this again — self-indulgence is not selfish. Taking care of yourself first allows you to be a better mom, wife, caregiver, business person, etc. In the interest of self-improvement, run the bath water, close the door to your bathroom, light some candles, put on some soft music, and don't forget to add some bubble bath (page 65), bath salts (page 64) or a few drops of your favorite essential oil. It's time to revive and refresh yourself!

Let's start by relaxing and entertaining this concept — saving money can be enjoyable and profitable. To prove this point, we are going to start with massage. Depending upon the spa you frequent, a massage can set you back $60 to $150. I am not saying you shouldn't treat yourself, but you can extend the treatment by a professional, or treat yourself if you don't have the money right now by making your own recipes. Relax, enjoy and dream about how good that massage will feel using these recipes Massage moves toxins from your body, increases blood flow, reduces stress and helps you relax.

*Massage therapists favor blends similar to this because of their ability to stay active on the skin for a longer time while they work with the muscle tissue. Over time, the oil will absorb into the skin and moisturize.*

## Deep-Tissue Massage Oil

**1 cup (237ml) sweet almond oil**
**¾ cup (177ml) apricot kernel oil**
**¼ cup (59ml) jojoba oil**
**2 tablespoons (30ml) coconut oil**
**4 to 15 drops essential oil (your preference and strength)**

Combine all the ingredients in a bottle and seal it tightly. Shake the bottle about 12 times so that the oils are well mixed. Store in a container labeled with name and make date.

Shelf Life: 3 to 5 months

A floral suspension in this formula will make a lovely bath oil or massage oil to give as a gift. Make sure you use freshly dried flowers like roses or lavender and healthy herbs such as rosemary. The flowers must be dried first and then cleaned of any pests or pesticides.

# European Nutrient Massage Oil

**4 ounces (118ml) olive oil**
**4 ounces (118ml) safflower oil**
**2 ounces (59ml) jojoba oil**
**3 to 15 drops essential oil (your preference and strength)**

Combine all the ingredients in a bottle and seal it tightly. Turn the bottle about 12 times so that the oils are well mixed. Store in a bottle labeled with name and make date.

Shelf Life: 3 to 5 months

## Tropical Massage Oil

**4 ounces (118ml) coconut oil**
**4 ounces (118ml) avocado oil**
**2 ounces (59ml) grape seed oil**
**3 to 15 drops essential oil (your preference and strength)**

Mix all the ingredients together. Store in a container labeled with name and make date.

Shelf Life: 3 to 5 months

## Massage Lotion

*This recipe calls for a purchased bottle of a thick hand or body cream. Use an inexpensive brand or a high-end cream. Your preference.*

**3 ounces (84ml) hand and body cream**
**1 ounce (28g) cocoa butter**

You may need to warm the cocoa butter first to make it soft, but don't melt it completely or you will need to stir the mix while it cools. Add into the hand and body cream and you'll have a consistency for massage. Store in a glass or plastic bottle. Label with name and make date.

Shelf Life: 2 to 3 months

# Massage Butter

½ cup (112g) shea or cocoa butter softened (can be partially heated)
1 tablespoon (14ml) grape seed oil
1 tablespoon (14ml) jojoba oil
1 teaspoon (5ml) vitamin E oil
Essential oil of your preference and strength

Soften the shea or cocoa butter. Add all other ingredients. Store in a plastic or glass container with lid. (You may need to warm and stir from time to time.) Label with name and make date.

Shelf Life: 9 to 12 months

*Shea butter or cocoa butter in a stick or brick form can be used in this recipe. The shea butter is a little harder to find. Try your local health food store.*

## Sore Muscle Massage Lotion

*For sore muscles, use any of the massage products and substitute the essential oil with eucalyptus and wintergreen oils.*

**Any massage product**
**2 drops eucalyptus essential oil**
**2 drops wintergreen oil**

Mix and store in a glass or plastic container. Label with name and make date.

Shelf Life: 9 to 12 months

## Pregnancy Anti-Stretch-Mark Rub

*What pregnant woman doesn't want to eliminate or prevent stretch marks?*

**½ cup (118ml) coconut oil**
**¼ cup (59ml) sweet almond or apricot kernel oil**
**¼ cup (59ml) grape seed oil**
**⅛ cup (30ml) jojoba oil or softened shea butter**
**1 tablespoon (15ml) calendula oil**
**Small amount of essential oil, unscented is better**

Mix all the oils together. Store in a glass or plastic container. Label with name and date.

Shelf Life: 3 to 5 months

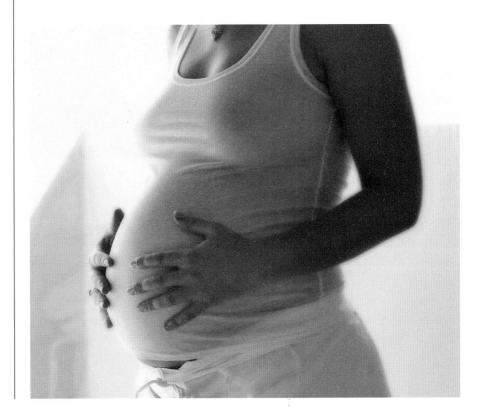

# BATHING BEAUTIES

Tub bathing should be a lovely "mini-vacation" — a relaxing, stress-free time when you can soak away your cares and troubles. Whether you choose a soak treatment or bubbles, make this occasion a time to relax and mindlessly drift away. Along with your bath treatment product, take your choice of weapons against stress — candles, soft music, aromatherapy, a book, etc.

## Relaxing Sea-Salt Bath Soak

**¼ cup (20g) sea salt or table salt**
**¼ cup (20g) Epsom salt**
**3 to 6 drops essential oil or your favorite perfume**

Mix the sea and Epsom salts. Use a spoon to stir in the small amount of oil until well dispersed.

Pour into your tub under running water and swirl around to mix. Store in a container labeled with name and make date.

Shelf Life: 1 year (Will keep longer if kept dry.)

*This recipe will help keep the bath water warmer for a longer time. Good quality sea salt contains healthy minerals for your body and the Epsom salt helps relax your muscles. Eventually, the fragrance may fade, but you can add more when needed.*

## Moisturizing Sea-Salt Bath Soak

**¼ cup (20g) sea salt or table salt**
**¼ cup (20g) Epsom salt**
**3 to 6 drops essential oil or your favorite perfume**
**1 tablespoon (15ml) oil of choice (apricot kernel, jojoba or sweet almond)**

Mix the sea and Epsom salt. Use a spoon to stir in the essential oil and the moisturizing oil. Stir until thoroughly blended. It will take a while and the crystals will look a bit wet. Pour into your tub under running water and swirl around to mix.

Shelf Life: 4 weeks (Excessive humidity will shorten the shelf life.)

*Add different oils to the recipe above. You'll get all the same benefits plus some wonderful moisturizing effects.*

## Bubble Bubble No Toil or Tro...

⅛ cup (30ml) liquid Castile soap
1 tablespoon (15ml) glycerin
3 to 6 drops essential oil or your favorite perfume

Mix together well with a spoon. Slowly pour under the running tap ...
a container labeled with name and make date.

Shelf Life: 6 months

## Nutritious Bath and Massage Oil

4 ounces (118ml) olive oil
4 ounces (118ml ) safflower oil
2 ounces (59ml) jojoba oil
3 to 15 drops essential oil (your preference and strength)

Mix all together and pour under running tap water. Soak and enjoy! Store in a container labeled with name and make date.

Shelf Life: 3 to 5 months

## Fizzy Fuzzy Bath

*Mix these two dry ingredients and then toss into your bath water. It will fizz for a few seconds then give you a soft and skin-nourishing bath. Use immediately.*

¼ cup (60g) powdered citric acid
¼ cup (32g) baking soda

## Butter

...13g) cocoa butter
...7g) coconut oil
...on (5ml) sweet almond oil
...ops essential oil (your choice)

...e cocoa butter in a double boiler on the stove. Add the coconut oil. When ...melted, remove from heat and add the sweet almond oil and essential oil. ...l it starts to cool (five minutes or so). Let setup (in the refrigerator, if you ...t in a decorative tin. Label with name and make date.

...e: 6 to 8 months

*more sweet almond oil until it stays soft when setup. If you're in a very hot climate and the butter stays melted all of the time, put it in the refrigerator to firm it up. The butter should be firm, yet you still should be able to spoon out a teaspoonful for your bath (it melts in the warm water).*

# SPA FACIAL MASKS

We all strive for toned fresh-looking skin and using a facial mask will help. The mask helps rejunvenate and tighten the skin, minimize large pores, remove dead skin layers and expose fresh, radiant skin. Treat your skin to a facial mask once a week for glowing results.

# Aloe and Milk Moisturizing Mask
## (for dry skin)

**½ cup (120g) aloe vera gel**
**¼ teaspoon (0.7g) cornstarch or arrowroot powder**
**1 teaspoon (5ml) milk of magnesia**

Mix together and apply to skin. Leave on skin for 10 to 15 minutes. Rinse off. Make and use immediately.

# Clay Facial Mask
## (for normal to oily skin)

**French or French green clay**
**Water**
**2 teaspoons (10ml) of your favorite oil (olive, sweet almond, avocado, etc.)**

Mix the clay with 50 percent water. Add the oil. Apply to your face. When the mask is completely dry on your skin, take it off. Make and use immediately.

*Milk of magnesia is great for your skin, plus it has a calming effect, as does the aloe vera gel.*

*You can buy French clay or French green clay at most health food stores. It works well for normal to oily skin, but not so great for dry skin. This mask will draw out the impurities in your skin, like black heads, whiteheads etc., making it great for troubled skin. By buying the clay and mixing it yourself, you won't have to fuss with preservatives or packaging and you'll save money over the commercial brand.*

## EASY AND FAST TIGHTENING MASK

Egg on her face? Yes, you heard me right...but not the whole egg. Egg whites do a great job of clarifying and tightening the skin! The white from one egg will usually be enough. I will let you compare the price to a professional skin-tightening mask from the spa. Amazing savings right? And the best part is — it really works!

Using one egg, separate the white from the yolk. Whip the egg white until stiff. Spread the whipped egg white on your freshly cleaned face (avoiding the eye area) and let sit. You will feel it tighten as it dries. Wash off with warm water. Tone and moisturize your skin.

# SCRUBS

Why scrub? When you are young, you scrub your face to remove extra bacteria and gently remove whiteheads, blackheads and pimples. When you are older, your natural skin exfoliation slows down. A scrub is a way to help the skin exfoliate (remove dead skin layers) and show off newer, fresher and less wrinkled skin. When you scrub, you do not want to pull hard on the skin (no stretching the skin please). Instead, use small, soft circular motions, doing small sections at a time. Do not scrub in one area longer than you can count to 10. A little scrubbing goes a long way. Scrub with your fingers or a washcloth. They do make facial brushes for this too, if you can find one in the cosmetic section of your store. These brushes are very soft.

## Tea Tree and Almond Meal Scrub
### (for normal to oily skin)

3 tablespoons (45ml) liquid Castile base for wash
4 drops tea tree oil or extract
2 tablespoons (28g) almond meal

Mix together and use fingers to gently scrub the skin. Rinse.

## Moisturizing Sugar Scrub

*The oil will not melt the sugar like water does, so you can use this wonderful scrub and add a bit of essential oil if you like.*

⅛ cup (25g) sugar
½ to 1 ounce (15ml to 30ml) oil (see what consistency you like best)

Mix and store in a container labeled with name and make date.

Shelf Life: 4 to 6 months

 **COST COMPARISON**
**Homemade: $0 .78 for 4 ounces**
**Salon Private Label: $7.99 for 4 ounces**

# ANTI-AGING

Several years ago, I was alone and having lunch at a cute little café. I had my book and a meal, the way many do when alone and grabbing a meal while on the road. Placing the book down to rest my eyes for a moment, I became aware of two darling mature women, probably in their mid-80s, sitting at the table next to mine. They were deep in conversation, and even though I did not want to eavesdrop, I could not help overhearing the following..."Well, I called her and asked why she could not come to lunch today, and she told me that she had too many aches and pains," said one woman. The other woman pondered for a moment and said, "You should have told her to come anyway. Getting old is not for wimps!" I giggled to myself and then realized how right she was. As we age, we do get aches and pains. So what happens to our skin as we age? The skin gets drier, the sebaceous oil glands slow production, our skin gets thinner as the subcutaneous fat shifts and leaves thin spots and sliding fat spots; skin gets less responsive, our sweat glands don't work as well in temperature changes, and our skin's ability (the melanin in our skin) to handle the sun decreases, producing uneven skin color. While a lift may be the solution for some of the more severe sagging caused from gravity and hormone shifts, some of these problems can be helped by our excellent homemade products. Let's address the following: age spots, puffy eyes, dry skin and dull appearance. Here we go....

## Amazing Results Home Face Lift (temporary)

*This recipe is based on other similar, effective, commercial spa treatments that I know. You can make this up at home and see the results for yourself.*

**4 ounces (118ml) distilled warm water**
**1 tablespoon (15g) pectin**
**1 egg white**
**⅛ teaspoon vitamin C crystals**
**¹/₁₆ teaspoon alum**
**3 drops menthol**

Whip egg white until stiff. Dissolve pectin, vitamin C and alum into warm water. Fold in egg white and menthol. Immediately, apply to your face and neck avoiding the eye area (mixture will be a little loose). Cover with warm towels or gauze and keep in place for 15 minutes. Put cool cucumbers over your eyes while you wait, if desired. Make and use immediately.

## Skin Lightener or Skin Bleach

*Little kids with freckles on their tiny upturned noses and soft bodies are very cute. Kiley and Carole, two young girls in my family, with their young "angel-kissed" faces (that's what we call their freckles) are adorable, but as we age those years of sun exposure and spots lose their cute appeal really fast. Use this recipe for age spots, freckles and uneven skin color. Spots with unfriendly names such as liver spots and age spots, sound much more gruesome. These are caused by the over-production of melanin and the spots can vary in size.*

*Lemon juice works to lighten skin and hair as effectively as "home-healthy bleach," but it needs an activator. Baking soda helps activate the bleaching process. This effective homemade recipe will help lighten freckles and age spots, although you will not see a lot of change after the first use. This recipe needs to be applied continually to see results over time, but it does work. It is not recommended for hair.*

**Juice from ½ fresh lemon**
**1 tablespoon (14g) baking soda**
**1 tablespoon (5g) powdered milk**

Mix the ingredients together. If too thick, use a few drops of distilled water to soften. Mixture should be like a paste. Apply to age spots or freckles. Leave on for five minutes. Wash off and apply moisturizer. Make and use immediately.

## Puffy Eye Help

If you have puffy eyes because of allergies, traveling or staying out late at night, try these solutions to get some relief.

Purchased gel-filled eye masks kept in the refrigerator can be used repeatedly. (Also good for sinus headaches.)

Wet green tea bags containing polyphenols and alkaloids
Chilled cucumber slices
Hemorrhoid suppositories work temporarily to shrink bags under the eyes

## Blemish Remover

For these troubled spots, dab a 50/50 blend of apple-cider vinegar and lemon juice to blemishes to help kill bacteria and reduce redness. Then, spread a small amount of honey on the blemish and cover with a band-aid. The honey helps retard the bacteria, forms a protective coating and soothes the area.

½ portion lemon juice
½ portion apple-cider vinegar
Honey

# EMERGENCY SKIN CARE GUIDE

Use this handy guide for quick answers to your personal care emergencies.

**Hemorrhoid suppositories:** bags under eyes

**Cucumber:** bags under eyes and as a toner

**Vegetable shortening:** eye make-up remover and skin cream

**Milk:** cleanser

**Milk of magnesia:** blemishes and poison oak

**Oatmeal:** rashes and sensitive skin

**Oil of oregano:** natural antiseptic

**Oil of peppermint and vanilla fragrance oil:** odors

**Tea tree oil:** natural antiseptic

**Listerine™ or other mouthwashes:** toner

**Lemon juice:** toner

**Apple cider:** sunburn

**Aspirin (salicylic acid):** acne breakouts

**Raw potato:** hot grease burns

**Potato juice:** natural toner

**Vodka or other clear alcohol:** dilute with water to use as toner or antiseptic

**Beer:** hair clarifier rinse

# OH, THEM FINGERS AND TOES!

*Have you ever had a paraffin dip at a professional spa? If you have, it is a treat and often it temporarily helps relieve aches and pains in the hands caused from arthritis. Now, you can make this at home. Double the recipe for treating your feet.*

*Here's how it works. The oil melts into the wax providing a moisturizing effect. As the beeswax dries on your skin, it tightens and forces the moisturizing oil into your skin. The warmth of the wax softens the skin and opens the pores, allowing maximum penetration of the oils trapped in your skin. This creates a very quick deep-therapy treatment for your hands or feet. A treat that will leave your hands and feet silky-soft, moisturized and pampered.*

Caution: Everyone's tolerance for heat is different. You want the wax hot, but not so hot it burns you. Make sure to test a small amount of wax before inserting your hand or foot.

## Paraffin Treat for Hands and Feet

**1 cup (228g) quality beeswax, block or chips**
**10 tablespoons (150ml) sweet almond oil**
**10 tablespoons (150ml) olive oil**

**Add: (your preference below or leave unscented)**
**4 drops comfrey or chamomile essential oil (for added softening)**
**3 drops oil of camphor**
**5 drops wintergreen oil (camphor and wintergreen for analgesic pain relief)**

Wax is flammable, so be sure to use a double boiler and melt slowly on low to medium heat. DO NOT LEAVE UNATTENDED. The recipe can be made firmer or softer by adjusting the oil or wax amounts.

When everything is melted, add to a pan that is deep enough to dip your hands or feet and allows for the recipe to cover them. For a hand treatment, do the following:

Thoroughly cleanse your hands.

Coat your hands with olive or sweet almond oil.

Quickly dip your hand into the warm (not scalding) wax solution with fingers slightly spread so the wax can flow around your fingers.

Remove your hand immediately after dipping.

Repeat two more times. Quickly dip and remove. This allows a thicker amount of wax to accumulate.

Repeat with your other hand.

Find a comfortable chair and relax until the wax cools (try to stay awake, this is pretty relaxing).

Here is the great part. When the wax is cool, peel off the wax and enjoy your soft beautiful hands.

Recycle the wax and use again.

Shelf Life: The wax will be good for up to one year. The reheating will cause the fragrance to dissipate, so add more essential oils every two to three treatments.

## Cuticle Softener

**1 tablespoon (15ml) grape seed oil**
**1 tablespoon (15ml) canola oil**
**1 each of vitamin A, D and E oil gel capsules**
**Optional: 1 drop essential oil**

Mix together the grape seed and canola oils. Pierce the gel capsules with a needle and squeeze the contents into the oil mix. Mix well. Store in a container labeled with name and make date.

Shelf Life: 1 month

*Rub this mixture on your cuticles and leave on for three to five minutes. Remove and use cuticle tool or cotton swab to push back and/or trim your cuticles. They will be soft and pliable and easy to work with. And, you have a choice — use the remaining product as a deep-therapy moisture treat for your hands or store your mix to use again.*

## Nail Polish Extender

**Favorite nail polish**
**Nail polish remover**

Add a few drops of the remover to your polish. Put cover back on and shake well.

*When your nail polish gets dry or thick and hard to apply, and you're ready to toss it, try and rescue it for more use. This little hint can extend the life of your favorite polish. The solvent added to the pigment used in nail polish evaporates over time. Adding a few drops of remover (also a solvent) re-moisturizes the existing pigment, unless it is so dry it has completely hardened.*

## Cheap and Easy Sore Foot Pedi-Soak

**2 tablespoons (37g) sea salt or table salt (sea salt is better)**
**½ cup (113g) Epsom salt**
**2 drops wintergreen oil or extract**
**2 drops peppermint oil or extract**

Add the sea and Epsom salts to the water. Stir in oil or extract. Store in a container labeled with name and make date.

Shelf Life: 3 to 5 months (Excessive humidity will shorten the shelf life.)

Legs get dry after shaving? Apply aloe vera gel for an easy after-shave soother.

*Soak away your troubles and ease your sore feet. Add this recipe to a foot soaker or an old roasting pan and fill with enough warm water to cover your feet. In the winter it will relax and warm you. In hot weather, use cool water.*

## Smelly Foot Spray

*Sweaty feet can be uncomfortable as well as smelly. This recipe will help prevent odor and keep your risk of foot fungus to a minimum.*

**4 ounces ( 120ml) water**
**3 to 4 drops wintergreen oil**
**3 to 4 drops eucalyptus oil**
**2 to 4 drops tea tree extract or oil**

Find a handy spray bottle. Add water and oils. Shake well. Label the bottle with name and make date.

Shelf Life: 1 to 2 months

## Foot Odor-Control Powder

*I started making this for my tennis shoes, as I liked to go barefoot in my tennis shoes during the summer. It worked really well, so I started making this in bulk. I use fabric scraps large enough to make a sachet. I put the powder in the middle of the fabric, gather it together and tie a ribbon around it. I toss the sachets in my husband's and son's sock drawers. I later found that I could stick these fabric sachets into their tennis shoes as an odor eater when they were not wearing them to work. You also can dust the powder right into the shoes. It not only will help with the odor, but the extra powder will absorb new perspiration created when they wear their shoes again. Tell them you are doing it for their comfort. (It is true, and it will keep their feet drier and more comfortable.) Do it, too, for the smell if they perform sweaty activities when wearing their tennis or work-out shoes.*

*Sprinkle in shoes when stored and before wearing. A wonderful foot odor/antiperspirant for the feet.*

**½ cup (64g) cornstarch (baking variety) (can substitute arrowroot powder or rice powder)**
**¼ cup (55g) baking soda**

Using a hand sifter, sift the cornstarch and baking soda together. Shake before using. Store in a container and label with name and make date.

Shelf Life: 6 months

Foot fungus problem? Add a few drops of tea tree oil to the powder. Put through a sifter a few times to mix in the oil. For aching feet, add and sift in a few drops of wintergreen oil and peppermint oil. As a simple shortcut, add the tea tree or wintergreen oil to baby powder.

# GLOSSING IT OVER

Make a lip gloss that you can carry in your purse. With this recipe, you can adjust the amount of shine and the firmness or softness of the lip gloss by simply increasing the amount of oil. (Oil makes it softer with more glide.) If it is too soft for you, add more beeswax in your next batch, or remelt the current batch and correct. The heat may damage your flavoring on a remelt, so add some more at that time. Small plastic, single-pill holders work well for storing the lip gloss.

# Lip Gloss

**1 tablespoon (15ml) melted beeswax**
**3½ tablespoons (49ml) oil (your choice olive, jojoba, apricot kernel oil or mix)**
**½ tablespoon (15g) aloe vera gel**
**4 to 6 drops flavoring (your favorite; the kind used for candy making)**
**Color (see notes below)**

Melt the beeswax and oil together in a small pan (double boiler is best) over low heat. The wax can become flammable if it gets too hot, so do not leave it unattended. As soon as melting occurs, remove from the heat. As the mixture cools, stir for about five minutes and as soon as the mixture starts to firm, whip in the aloe vera gel using rapid strokes for about one minute. Add the flavor (and color). While the mixture cools, keep stirring until it is thick enough to stay together. Transfer into little lip-gloss pots or similar container.

Combine more than one flavoring when adding the six drops.

To add color to your lip gloss, use children's nontoxic color crayons. Add the color shavings late in the melting stage and voila! – colored, flavored lip balm. Food coloring is water based and cannot be used it in this recipe. In commercial formulas we also use a wax-based color.

# CROWNING GLORY HAIR CARE

## SHAMPOOS

*Use this recipe to form a base shampoo. This base recipe can be used to craft other custom shampoos.*

### Gentle Basic Shampoo

**6 ounces (180ml) liquid Castile soap (store-bought or homemade, page 50)**
**6 ounces (180ml) distilled water**

Mix well. Store in bottle and label with name and make date.

Shelf Life: 6 months

### Alternative Basic Shampoo

**2 to 4 ounces (56g to 112g) unscented clear glycerin soap**
**2 to 4 ounces (60ml to 120ml) distilled water**

Place the soap in a double boiler over low heat. Heat slowly and do not let it come to a boil. When the soap is melted, add the distilled water to make a gentle shampoo. Not all companies make their soap the same. If the mixture is too thick, remelt and add more water until it is a thin liquid-gel consistency.

### Custom Basic Shampoo
(for dry hair or scalp)

*These two oils work best with the basic shampoo recipe. They're also great for moisturizing the scalp.*

**To every 6 to 8 ounces (180ml to 240ml) of basic shampoo add:**
**1 teaspoon (5ml) grape seed oil or jojoba oil**

Shake before using, as oil may settle from time to time. Store in a container labeled with name and make date.

Shelf Life: 2 to 3 months

## Custom Salicylic Acid Shampoo

(for dandruff control)

*There are several ways to treat dandruff – here are two recipes. If you look at commercial dandruff treatments you will see that many treatments contain salicylic acid. Guess what that is? — aspirin. Now that you know, you can make your own salicylic acid dandruff shampoo. Shampoo and leave on for three to five minutes, then shampoo again and rinse thoroughly.*

**6 to 8 ounces (180ml to 240ml) basic shampoo, page 81**

**3 to 4 crushed aspirin**

**3 to 4 tablespoons (45ml to 60ml) water**

Crush the aspirin. Liquefy the aspirin by dissolving in the water. Add it to the base shampoo or your favorite shampoo. Store in a new/reused container if not adding to your purchased shampoo. Label the container with name and make date.

Shelf Life: 3 to 4 months

## Tea Tree, Rosemary and Ginger (*Awapuhi*) Shampoo

*If you have dandruff or oily hair, use this shampoo. These ingredients tone the scalp, rid your hair of oil and slow down new oil production.*

**6 to 8 ounces (180ml to 240ml) basic shampoo, page 81**

**14 to 16 drops oil or extract (one or a combination)**

      **6 drops tea tree extract**

      **4 drops rosemary extract**

      **4 drops ginger essential oil**

Mix oil with basic shampoo. Store in container labeled with name and make date. Shake well before using.

Shelf Life: 6 months

## Color-Extending Hair Shampoo

*For centuries, plant ingredients have been used as dye bases and colorants. Cave men even used herbs to rub color into some of their cave drawings. Now, upscale salons are selling color-enhancing shampoos. Many of them contain herbs that support the color of the hair and add shine. Here is a way you can make your own. Match the following herbs to your hair color.*

**Herbs of your choosing:**

**Blond: yarrow or chamomile**

**Brunette: black malva flowers and rosemary**

**Red: red sage or madder root**

**Small amount of water**

**1 tablespoon (30ml) herb color-support juice\***

**6 ounces (180ml) shampoo (your choice)**

\*Place the herbs in a pot with a very small amount of water. Place a lid on the pot. Bring the water to a boil. Turn down to low and simmer (with lid) for 30 minutes. There will not be a lot of color and it does not work like a dye. It is color support and extra shine. Add the colored liquid to your shampoo of choice. Shake occasionally. Label the bottle with name and make date.

Shelf Life: 1 to 2 months

## Natural Hair Color

Henna is a natural ingredient that is derived from the bark of a tree. It is very strong and can be found at many health food stores. It is used for hair tinting and applying to the skin for non-permanent tattoos. You do not have a lot of control with this product, but if you want to try it, make sure you get some with directions as there are different Henna colors. Look for one that is suitable to the color you desire. Henna also tends to make your hair look thicker.

## Volumizing Shampoo

*Don't drink that beer — add it to the basic shampoo! Beer will pump up the volume and put shine in your hair. It also temporarily helps expand the hair shaft.*

**2 ounces ( 120ml) beer**
**6 ounces (180ml) basic shampoo, page 81**

Add beer to shampoo. Store in a glass or plastic bottle. Occasionally, shake the bottle to keep mixed. Label bottle with name and make date.

Shelf Life: 1 month

## Natural Deep-Therapy Hair Treatment

*Once in awhile, your hair needs a good spa treatment. Once a month or so, create this tasty treat for your hair. The gelatin provides the hair with protein, the oils add luster and the avocado provides conditioning "fats" that nourish your hair. After shampooing, work treatment into your hair. It's also great for the scalp. Leave on five minutes then rinse thoroughly. Enjoy your soft full hair!*

**½ avocado peeled and mashed**
**2 tablespoons (30ml) favorite oil (olive, grape seed, jojoba or similar)**
**1 tablespoon (30g) unflavored gelatin**
**1 ounce (30ml) water**

Dissolve gelatin in water (will be like jelly). Mash all together. If too thick, add more water, but you want it somewhat thick. Use immediately.

# WHERE DID YOU GET THOSE PEARLY WHITES?

## MOUTH AND TOOTH CARE

### Homemade Toothpaste

*Baking soda will clean the teeth, lemon is used for whitening and the peppermint freshens your mouth.*

**¼ teaspoon (1.2ml) lemon juice**
**⅛ cup (29g) baking soda**
**1 drop peppermint extract**
**Water to make a paste**

Make and use immediately.

### Treatment for Sore Gums and Sore Throat

*Use as a gargle or for rinsing sore gums.*

**1 tablespoon (19g) salt**
**2 ounces (60ml) warm water**

Mix well. Make and use immediately.

### Canker Sore Relief

*Your pharmacist will know what sweet oil is, or you can find it at health food stores. It is a very pure form of olive oil and is used for pure bases in pharmacology. Buy it in small amounts over the counter or by request without a prescription from your pharmacist. Apply a drop two times a day to the canker sore for fast healing and pain relief.*

**1 teaspoon (1ml) sweet oil**
**1 drop camphor**
**1 drop tea tree oil**

Mix all the ingredients together. Store in a bottle labeled with name and make date.

Shelf Life: 6 months

## Tooth Whitener

Caution: Do not use this as a daily toothpaste. Hydrogen peroxide can kill good bacteria as well as bad so limit this whitening to one to two times a week.

**⅛ teaspoon (1ml) hydrogen peroxide**
**½ cup (120ml) water**
**⅓ cup (74g) baking soda**

Add the baking soda to the water and hydrogen peroxide mix to make a light paste. Brush with your toothbrush. Use immediately.

## Mouthwash

*You need to be of drinking age to use this mouthwash recipe. But if you read the ingredients on most mouthwashes, they have a form of alcohol in them. If you do not drink, its OK. Remember, you are rinsing and spitting, not drinking. Rinse again. Alcohol does kill germs.*

**2 ounces (60ml) vodka or Everclear (no taste or odor)**
**2 ounces (60ml) water**
**3 drops tea tree extract**
**Water-soluble peppermint or cinnamon flavoring**

Dissolve the flavoring into the vodka or Everclear. Add water. This is a mouthwash – do not drink. Store in a bottle and label with name and make date.

Shelf Life: 4 to 5 months

## Non-Alcoholic Mouthwash

**2 ounces (60ml) white vinegar**
**2 ounces (40ml) water**
**½ teaspoon (3g) baking soda**
**3 drops tea tree oil**
**Flavoring of your choice (peppermint or cinnamon is nice)**

Mix all together and use immediately.

Use flavored vodka and just add water for a simple and easy mouthwash.

# FOR THE KIDS

Kids and grandkids...we love to smell their hair, tickle their toes and make them smile.
The following are kid pleasers and solutions for all the "little treasures" in your life.

# POWDERS AND BUBBLES

*Who's the baby? This recipe makes a lovely powder and it's much safer than talc. Create a batch and divide it up — some for baby, some for you. Double or triple the recipe and you'll have plenty to use and give as gifts. Additional fragrance can be added in later if you decide you want a stronger smell.*

## Soft Dusting Powder for Baby and You

**1 cup (128g) cornstarch**
**1 cup (158g) rice flour**
**Essential oil if desired**

Sift together the cornstarch and rice flour. Add essential oil, if desired. If adding fragrance, sift it two to three times to force the fragrance in. Then, put it into a decorative tin with a big puff, or an empty shaker. Label with name and make date.

Shelf Life: 6 to 12 months

## Beary Nice Bath Crystals for Kids

**½ cup (114g) Epsom salt**
**½ cup (84g) sea salt**
**Few drops food coloring (your choice)**
**Few drops fragrance (your choice)**

Mix the Epsom salt and the sea salt. Add a few drops of food color for fun and a few drops of a fragrance they love. Mix well to saturate the salt with color. Add about two tablespoons per bath.

*Use leftover plastic honey bear jars to store the bath crystals. It makes a cute colored bear with a smelly belly. After the fragrant crystals are in the bear, you'll find the kids sneaking into the bathroom to smell the bear's belly when you aren't looking. That's why I call them smelly-belly crystals. The Epsom salt keeps the water warmer longer and it helps soften hard water. Also useful to help relax wound-up kids before bed. Epsom salt (pure magnesium sulfate) helps relax the muscles.*

# Simple Bath Bubbles

*Let the bubbles and fun begin. Put this mix in an empty plastic honey bear, too — another smelly belly. How about a duo pack for a holiday surprise?*

**6 ounces (180ml) liquid Castile soap, page 50**
**1 tablespoon (15ml) glycerin**
**Few drops essential oil (your child's favorite smell)**

Mix and store in container of choice. Label with name and date. Add one to two tablespoons (15ml to 30ml) to the bath under running tap water.

Shelf Life: 3 to 6 months

---

## TANGLE TROUBLE
A little bit of mayonnaise works as a hair de-tangler and conditioner. While the little tyke is still in the bath or shower, work a tablespoon of mayonnaise into the hair and leave on for a minute. Use a big-tooth comb to comb through the hair and remove snarls. Rinse well. Leaves a great shine and it does not burn the eyes.

---

# Nursery Air Freshener

*Clear up those not-so-nice smells and freshen the babies' or kids' rooms — or any room in the house. It's fun to have a few different scents. Maybe one as a closet freshener, a room freshener, kid's room, etc. If you are using in a nursery, vanilla is best to cut urine smell in diaper pails, otherwise choose any fresh or citrus scent.*

**4 ounces (120ml) distilled water**
**4 ounces (120ml) vodka**
**1 teaspoon (5ml) essential oil**

Put into a small spray bottle and shake well. Label with name and make date.

Shelf Life: 3 to 4 months

# SAVE BIG DOLLARS ON SCENTS!

## ESSENTIAL OILS AND PERFUMES

Here is a way to extract the "essence" of flowers, herbs, citrus and spices. Soak a large amount of the product you are extracting in a small amount of natural oil. I will explain the process to you and give you a sample formula to try. Once you understand the process, you will be able to make many kinds of essential oils. This is a home formula, and though it will be potent, some commercial distillation processes make a commercial product stronger than your home-based oil.

Always start with fresh ingredients. Old or dried herbs and flowers will not work for this process. When working with flowers, use "meaty" flowers like roses, lilacs or jasmine. There is plenty of fiber in them to transfer into the oil. Citrus peels, most herbs and vanilla bean also are great choices. Glass jars, such as recycled mayonnaise or pickle jars, work great for this process. DO NOT USE PLASTIC JARS!

### Essential Oil

**4 to 6 cups flower petals, herbs, spices or citrus peels**
**8 ounces (240ml) carrier oil (almond oil, apricot oil or jojoba oil)**

You may need to adjust the amount of carrier oil depending on the product you are extracting. You always want to use the least amount of carrier oil possible.

Using your hands or a mortar and pestle, lightly "bruise" the material you are extracting. This will open up the fibers and start the "bleeding" of the plant.

Place the "bruised materials" into your glass jar.

Add just enough oil to cover the materials, using the least amount possible while still covering the material.

Put the lid on the jar and shake or swirl.

Now comes the waiting, the rest will happen without you.

Store this jar in a cool, dark place for about a month.

Take it out weekly, if you remember, and swirl or shake once and then put it back. This makes the scent stronger. If you do forget, the processing will continue. During this waiting process, the "essence" or smell of the material is bleeding and fermenting into the oil. The essence will get stronger and stronger until it eventually becomes an essential oil.

At the end of the month, strain off the material.

Pour the new essential oil into a small (glass only) vial. Label your oils with name and make date.

Shelf Life: 6 months

# Perfume Oil

To make a perfume oil, use a homemade or purchased bottle of an essential oil. Use glass jars (never use plastic) for storing your essential oil or perfume. Eyedroppers are necessary when using oils in your recipes.

**6 to 25 drops essential oil (lesser amount if commercial grade, higher amount if homemade)**
**2 to 3 ounces (60ml to 90ml) sweet almond oil, jojoba oil or grape seed oil**

Add oils together and mix. Store in glass container labeled with name and make date.

Shelf Life: 6 months

# Classic Perfume

**6 to 25 drops homemade or commercial essential oil**
**2 to 3 ounces (60ml to 90ml) vodka or Everclear**

Using an eyedropper, add the essential oil to the vodka or Everclear. Mix well. Store in a glass container labeled with name and make date.

Shelf Life: 6 months

## FRAGRANCE DOS AND DON'TS

Avoid storing your oils and fragrances in heat and sunlight. This can damage the delicate balance of essential oils and extracts. Store in a dark container, if possible, in a cool dark place. Do not apply fragrance to silk or other fabrics that may stain, and do not use on polished furniture items.

Cinnamon is a fairly caustic spice. Once, I made a strong essential oil from cinnamon sticks using the same process for making essential oil. I put some on a grease stain on the concrete in our garage and overnight it ate right through the stain and cleaned it up. Amazing!

# CHAPTER TWO
# FEELING BETTER NATURALLY

It is important, at some point, that we pay attention to the purification of the very basic needs in our existence. I am sure we all agree that we deserve the best when it comes to the basics. Clean air, clean water, and food without lingering pesticides. These are the necessary tools we must have to build our foundation of health. I will not discuss foods in this book, but do look for my companion book, "Quick-Fix Healthy Mix." Due for release in spring of 2010, this book will show you how to make foods in bulk that are inexpensive, healthy and save you time.

The air inside our homes can be two to four times more polluted than the air outside. Yes, you heard me right. We worry about pollution outside, and yet, we come home to our sanctuary to find it more polluted.

# CLEAN AIR

Some of the more common sources of indoor air pollution are VOCs (volatile organic compounds). VOCs come from cleaning products, pesticide residue and out-gassing from painted walls, furniture, carpets, etc. These substances can stay in the air in your home and cause a range of health problems from allergies, headaches and simple nausea, to ongoing diseases or much worse.

## SOLUTIONS FOR HOME POLLUTANTS

Making your own less toxic products and buying green cleaning products are ways to get started.

Even a well-insulated home that's energy efficient needs some ventilation so that there is a clean air/dirty air exchange. Talk to an energy specialist, usually for free, at your local electric or gas company.

**Following are easy ideas to improve the air quality in your home to help make it eco-friendly:**

- Avoid furniture and flooring made with formaldehyde.

- When it comes time to paint, choose low VOC paint. It is available and affordable.

- Indoor plants (see page 161) can improve air quality inside your home as plants convert carbon dioxide to oxygen and help clean the air.

- Keep dust at a minimum, this means dusting from the top down. The first time you do this, begin with dusting the high places and then move down through the room, vacuuming last. Then, guess what, do it again one more time — yes, the whole cycle. Once a week, zip through the same procedure. You only have to do it twice the first time. Then, do it again every six months to keep dust build-up to a minimum in hard to reach places.

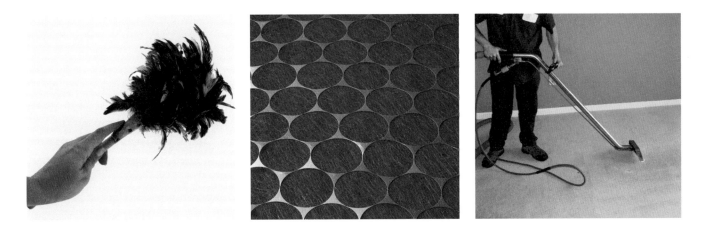

Clean your air filters. When I worked in the medical field, we had a woman that professed she was a "clean freak," but she had constant allergy problems in the winter. After a lot of testing, we only could find dust and mold allergies. She insisted that she only had hardwood floors and that she kept her house very dust free. Finally, one of the staff asked her how often she cleaned the dust filters on her furnace? She answered, "What filters?" So, we sent her back home. She discovered that she did have air filters and they were a dirty, nasty mess. She changed the filters and her "winter" allergies, when she ran her furnace, got a lot better. Every time she ran the furnace, she was circulating the air through old nasty filters. Don't let this be you; change your air filters every six months.

If you have an electronic air filter, remove the filter and wash it per the manufacturer's instructions. Usually, it should be washed every month so that it works efficiently. Personally, I would not be without my internal air filter and de-ionizer. If you are building or buying a new furnace, you can order the furnace with the electronic air cleaner built in as an additional air cleaner. If not, there are several smaller room-by-room or whole-house air cleaners that make a splendid addition to your indoor air quality.

Control the dirt and dust in your home. In Hawaii, I learned to take off my shoes before entering my home. A lot of dirt and grime is tracked onto your floors via your "outside shoes." Why not keep a shoe tray by the door and remove your shoes as you enter. You'll have less dust, dirt, and grime to clean.

Use HEPA vacuum cleaners or filters. Vacuum cleaners suck up the dirt, and with the suction, where does the air go? Well, back into your air. Most of the dirt stays in the bag, but depending on the quality of your vacuum, some of it is flying right back at you. A good vacuum is worth the price. It is recommended that you deep clean (steam clean) your carpets at least once a year to keep them hygienic (twice a year is better). If you need motivation for this, see the section on dust mites, page 96. Use steam cleaners or make your own cleaning products instead of using chemical cleaners. The prices have come down on little steam cleaners and they clean flooring, counters and furniture without chemicals. Use it for a deeper clean to complement your homemade cleaning supplies.

Need rags? Use old cloth diapers. They can be used over and over again and you won't get the "paper dust" from paper towels.

# CLEAN WATER

Whether you have city water, well water or some sort of a catchment system, "stuff" is getting into your water supply. Some of the contaminants are naturally occurring, and in small amounts may be good for you, such as natural minerals like iron, sulfur and manganese, although they can play havoc with your laundry colors. We have known about and have been addressing the previous particles in our water for a long time. Other than the inconvenience of minerals in the water, usually called hard water, there are a lot more concerns now about our water quality. So much so, the government has established parts per million (ppm) acceptability standards for water. The government understands that they no longer can expect water to be untainted by some pollutants so they are allowing minuscule portions of pollutants in the water.

These pollutants include not only naturally occurring minerals and rust residue from aging pipes, but also pollutants from runoff, such as pesticides, pharmaceuticals, bacteria, sediments, plant and animal "matter," algae....Well, you get the picture.

Each year, your public works department will publish or make available their report on local water. In the report, there should be a breakdown of "ppm" for what's in your water and include a comparison to the national standards. If you don't have public water, you will need to call someone to come and analyze your water. Look in your yellow pages or on the Internet under "water treatment" for contact information.

There are two basic components to treating water. One is filtering and the other is softening. Filtering uses a variety of methods depending on your water scores. A simple carbon filter will work for most households. The filtering process is tailored to remove organic chemicals, inorganic chemicals and microbiological organisms found in your water. The softening helps remove chlorine, salt and minerals. The removal of these chemicals will help save your bathroom fixtures and enable you to use about one-half of the soap or cleaners you are using if you have hard water. It also saves you money and helps you become more environmentally responsible.

Many companies will come out and test your water for free, as you may be a potential customer. To request or obtain your water report, call your city or public works department or call a water treatment company and request a free test.

# DUST MITES

These nasty little creatures cause you the most concern in your bedding and they are microscopic, so don't try to look for them. As nasty as they are, everyone has them. All creatures have tiny organisms that live off the waste from their bodies. Dust mites eat dead skin cells from people and pets.

Now that I am through making you uncomfortable, I will tell you again, cleanliness is next to Godliness. The mites live on the surface of your bedding and sometimes in your flooring. They easily are killed with hot water and soap, so when you wash your sheets (at least once a week please) or you steam clean and vacuum your carpets, you eliminate most of them. Some of us, myself included, have allergic reactions to an abundance of these — so keep those sheets clean. For those especially vulnerable, a switch from carpet to hardwoods or other fiber-free floor surfaces will help. Just to let you know, most people are not allergic to the mites in particular as much as the feces that the mites produce. In a used mattress or pillow that has not been protected with covers (available at the allergy store) there can be nearly 100,000 mites living in one square foot area. Each mite can produce up to 20 waste droppings per day. You can buy plastic covers (they have new, soft plastic that does not make crunchy noises when you sleep on it) for your bed and pillows so that you do not saturate your mattress.

Keeping your internal house temperature below 70°F (21°C) is another way to prevent dust mites. Dust mites love warm moist areas (just as mold does). Use air filters for better air quality.

Remember to wash often and use allergy covers to control your exposure to the dust mites and their feces.

# SIMPLE HOME REMEDIES FOR MINOR AILMENTS

With the increased popularity of essential oils and herbal remedies, it's not unusual for more people to be thinking about what's natural and what's not.

Herbal therapies have been used by early alchemists for pharmacological purposes since the beginning of recorded time. We are still discovering, even today, plants in the rainforests that have new applications and rediscovering ancient uses for plants. Not all knowledge has been recorded and handed down. It also is a well-known fact that many plants, herbs and flowers are the basis of some of the strong pharmaceutical drugs on the market. With traditional medicinal costs skyrocketing, and more and more concerns about drug safety and side effects, alternative medicine has stepped forward as less of an alternative and more of a viable resource for gaining and maintaining health.

I am offering you the following solutions to minor problems inconveniencies. For serious illness, or if you are on medications, it would be prudent to check with your primary health care provider as the use of some herbs can interfere with certain medications.

I want to share with you some self-help recipes for everyday life that you can make at home. Sometimes, you want to comfort yourself from those little inconveniences. Like everywhere in this book, the goal is help you control costs and feel safe, knowing the materials used in these recipes are simple, natural ingredients that you have in your own home. Picture this comfort from yesteryear...homemade cough syrup and a bowl of chicken soup delivered to a home-bound friend with the flu, or serving it at home to a loved one (maybe even yourself). The act of caring, wholesome and homemade recipes served with a hug or smile —what could be a better comfort?

## Apple-Cider Vinegar and Honey Internal Toner

**1 teaspoon (5ml) honey**
**1 teaspoon (5ml) apple-cider vinegar**
**8 ounces (240ml) hot water**

Stir the honey and apple-cider vinegar into hot water.
Drink one glass everyday. Use immediately.

*..help your body balance itself by providing both acid and alkali. I recently walked through a health food store and saw a NEW miracle cure that was advertised as a "special internal cleansing and toning product" to help the body achieve balance and heal itself. Guess what it was?..a pill made from apple-cider vinegar and honey. Why buy a pill and pay for the packaging when you can make this as a tea for pennies?*

## Gentle and Healthy Vegetable Laxative

**8 ounces (240ml) tomato juice**
**4 ounces (120ml) carrot juice**
**4 ounces apple (120ml) juice**
**4 ounces sauerkraut (120ml) juice**

Mix juices in a container. Keep in the refrigerator. Shake or stir before drinking to mix evenly.

Shelf Life: 2 to 3 days

*This works pretty fast and it's good for you. I know someone with irritable bowl syndrome (IBS) that swears this drink keeps her stabilized and regular. Don't forget to drink at least four to six glasses of water a day.*

## Upset Tummy and Indigestion Relief

*Papaya is full of pepsin which helps get digestion back on track. When buying pepsin capsules, it is important to buy the gel types so that you can open and pour them into the mix. (Many of the commercial tablets are made from calcium carbonate.) Acidophilus naturally occurs in your body in the form of friendly bacteria and it's also found in yogurt. Ginger or a small drop of peppermint soothes an upset tummy. Together, they provide relief. Sip on this drink to help get the tummy settled and back on track.*

*If you can find a supplier who sells straight calcium carbonate, you can take ½ teaspoon (3g) of the powder every four hours on a temporary basis for a big cost savings. It will taste chalky, so you might want to mix it in a small amount of juice.*

8 ounces (240ml) lemon-lime carbonated soda
1 pepsin gel capsule
1 acidophilus gel capsule
4 ounces (120ml) concentrated ginger tea
1 drop peppermint oil

Open the pepsin and acidophilus capsules and pour into the ginger tea. Add peppermint oil. Mix together and stir well. Use immediately.

### QUICK AND INEXPENSIVE FIXES TO AN UPSET STOMACH INCLUDE:

· Ginger-ale soda and ginger tea with a drop of peppermint.

· Try to keep acidophilus and pepsin capsules on hand. Take one for an upset stomach or use the recipe above.

# BAD BREATH

Pepsin and comfrey pills help clear the acids in your stomach which sometimes can affect your breath. Also, liquid chlorophyll diluted in water or taken in pill form helps with bad breath. Check bottles for shelf life. Chlorophyll is found naturally in many greens and is nature's way to help clean up the body. Pepsin can be found in most health food stores. See make your own mouthwash, page 86.

# BOILS

*Fresh sliced tomato or concentrated tomato paste can be placed on boils. Acids from the tomatoes help soothe and bring the boils to a head for quicker healing. For a stronger poultice, use the Boil Poultice recipe.*

## Boil Poultice

**1 tablespoon (14g) alum**
**2 ounces (60ml) pure uncooked tomato juice**
**Gauze or cloth pad**

Dissolve the alum into the tomato juice. Apply the mix directly to the boil. Cover with gauze and let sit for 15 minutes. Wash off. Make and use immediately.

# BURNS

If you accidentally burn a small area of your body with high heat, particularly stove or oven burns, this remedy works amazingly well. Immediately following the burn, run cold water over the burn to "quick cool." Cut a fresh potato in half and place the cut end of the potato on the burn. The fresh juice from the potato contains a starch enzyme that helps relieve the pain and calm the skin. Once the pain is controlled, apply an antiseptic. Follow with aloe vera gel.

Colgate™ toothpaste makes a quick salve for burns. The paste formula seems to work better than the gel formula.

*If you immediately see sunburn developing, straight apple-cider vinegar is amazing! It will not stop the burn from developing, but it will minimize the amount of pain you experience during the healing process. Saturate the area by dabbing on straight apple-cider vinegar every 15 to 20 minutes until the sunburn develops. However, you will smell like a salad dressing. Once the burn is developed, switch from the straight vinegar to the Sunburn Calmer for soothing relief.*

## Sunburn Calmer

**1 ounce (29g) aloe vera gel**
**1 ounce (29g) plain unflavored yogurt**
**1 ounce (30ml) apple-cider vinegar**

Mix together and use two to three times a day. Dab it on and let it dry to calm irritated burnt skin. Stir before each use.

Shelf Life: 4 days to 1 week — Keep in the refrigerator.

**COST COMPARISON**
**Homemade: $3.36 for 6 ounces**
**Burt's Bee's: $10.99 for 6 ounces**

# BUG BITES AND STINGS

The painful irritation usually is caused by either a small amount of venom left in the skin or by the injury reaction to a bite.

*If you're bitten by a bug, cleanse the area and quickly apply ice. It will help numb the area and reduce the initial swelling. Once you remove the ice, use the following recipes.*

Follow the instructions at right for Bite Be Gone, and if you do not have the ingredients (oils) for the second application, occasionally rub a hemorrhoid suppository (made with shark oil to relieve swelling and itching) over the area. It also will help calm down swelling. Follow with plain aloe vera gel for soothing.

## Bite Be Gone

**Baking powder or baking soda**
**Water**

Make a 50/50 paste with the water and baking powder. Place mix on the bite or sting. Discard any additional mixture.

Once you have calmed down the majority of the redness and irritation with the above recipe, grab some aloe vera gel and make up the following. For the next day or two, occasionally apply this mixture for additional relief (especially for itching). Essential oils can be added for additional calming.

**1 tablespoon (20g) aloe vera gel**
**1 teaspoon (5ml) sweet oil**
**Optional: Few drops essential oil (lavender or chamomile)**

Shelf Life: 4 days to 1 week

## Minor Wound Antiseptic Cleanser

*This is a cost-savings shortcut that will help you extend your more expensive antiseptic products and still get the job done. Mix it up in advance so you have some ready when you need it.*

**2 teaspoons (10ml) iodine**
**2 ounces (60ml) isopropyl alcohol**
**1 teaspoon (5ml) tea tree extract**
**1 ounce (30ml) distilled water**

Mix all the ingredients together. Store in a bottle and label with name and make date.

Shelf Life: 18 months to 2 years

# BRUISES

Arnica tablets, available at health food stores, will cut the healing time on bruising. Many plastic surgeons recommend that their patients take Arnica for a few days before surgery as it dramatically speeds up healing from bruising. Keep it on hand in your "natural" medicine chest. It helps everyday bumps and bruises go away faster too. See label for shelf life.

# HEADACHE

I learned a simple quick cure for a headache from my grandfather, a naturopathic doctor. There is a special spot located in the apex of the soft skin on your hand where your thumb and first finger meet. Applying pressure to this area with the thumb and first finger of your other hand in the correct area works like magic!

For frontal headaches or whole-head headaches, take turns applying pressure, first to one hand then the other. If your headache is more temporal (on the side) for your right side, apply the pressure to your left hand, if your headache is more on the left side, work your right hand.

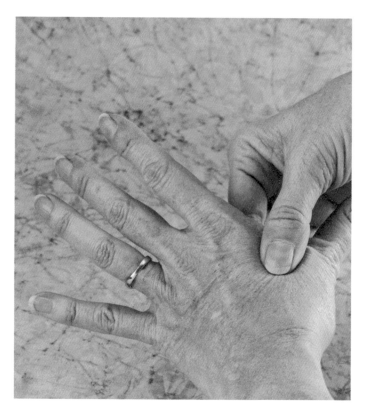

*The herbs listed at right combine analgesic, calming, alkalizing, anti-inflammatory and decongestant properties that are useful for headaches. Make a homemade ready-to-use headache recipe by combining equal amounts of these herbs.*

## Herbal Headache Relief

**Make a tea with equal amounts of each herb**
**Chamomile**
**Comfrey**
**Lemon balm**

Drink the tea and relax. Use immediately.

# SORE THROAT, COLDS AND COUGHS

Scratchy or sore throats result from an irritation of the mucus membranes in the throat. To soothe and help settle the irritation, the throat needs to be coated in a pleasant way. Here is a homemade sore throat and cough drop you can make and give as a gift during the cold season. Remember when Julie Andrews sang, "A spoonful of sugar makes the medicine go down?" Sugar works great in cough drops. The sugar and honey combination temporarily coats and soothes the throat. The lemon helps clear the phlegm and open the passageway. Similar formulas to this recipe are still found today in many commercial cough drops, but why not save money and make your own? I am giving you a "master" formula. In the recipes for cough drops and cough syrup, you can substitute the lemon extract or juice with any of the following: horehound or chamomile extract for soothing, wintergreen extract for cooling and clearing sinuses, or any other of your choice. WHATEVER YOU CHOOSE, BE SAFE AND MAKE SURE IT IS FOOD GRADE.

Zinc and vitamin C tablets help soothe a sore throat. Chew up the vitamin C tablet, then suck slowly on the zinc tablet. Afterward, make and drink some echinacea tea.

# Basic Cough Drops

1¾ cups (350g) sugar (or sugar equivalent for sugar free)
2 ounces (57g) honey
6 ounces (170g) light corn syrup
½ teaspoon (2.5ml) lemon extract
4 ounces water (120ml) water

Line a 9" x 9" (23cm x 23cm) baking pan with aluminum foil, covering both the bottom and sides of the pan.

Butter the inside of a two-quart (2L) saucepan.

Combine the sugar, corn syrup, water, and honey in the pan.

Cook and stir over medium-high heat until the mixture boils, stirring constantly to dissolve the sugar (about four to six minutes).

Turn the heat down to medium and continue a light boil at a steady rate, stirring occasionally until a candy thermometer reads 290°F (143°C) (soft crack stage). Continue to cook for 20 minutes, stirring occasionally.

Remove from heat and let cool; over the next two to three minutes, stir occasionally.

Add the lemon and other herbs and vitamins, if desired.

Immediately, pour into the foil-lined pan to cool; over the next two to three minutes, stir occasionally.

As it cools another three to 10 minutes, use a spatula to mark your break lines into the cough drop mixture. Make squares into the desired serving size.

The marks will stay when the mixture is set. If your marks do not stay, the mix is still too hot and needs to cool more. Try again in a few minutes.

Let set overnight. Use foil to lift cough drop mixture out of the pan. Break along the marks. If not perfect in shape, don't worry, they will soothe your throat just fine.

Package in little cut squares of plastic wrap, or you can buy candy wrappers at cake-decorating stores or in the candy-crafting sections at craft or grocery stores.

Store in a small plastic bag or pretty paper sack until needed and place in a cool dark place.

Yield: Approx. 150 squares (depending on your size of cuts)

Shelf Life: Up to 6 months if properly wrapped and stored

**$** **COST COMPARISON**
**Homemade: $0.95 for 20 homemade drops**
**Cepacol™ Sore Throat Cough Drops: $3.79 for 18 drops**

## Nighttime Lemon and Honey Cold and Cough Syrup

*Most cough syrups have alcohol as a cough silencer and this recipe will work like most others. Maybe you will sleep soundly as well. One to two teaspoons before bed and... nighty night.*

2 ounces (57g) honey
2 tablespoons (30ml) lemon juice
2 tablespoons (30ml) liquid glycerin
1 ounce (30ml) vodka

Warm the honey until it liquefies. When honey is not too hot, add in the other ingredients. Mix well. Store in a bottle labeled with name and make date. Keep out of the reach of children.

Shelf Life: 6 months

**$ COST COMPARISON**
**Homemade: $1.80 for 4 ounces**
**Natural B & T Brand™ : $7.49 for 4 ounces**

## Canker Sore Soother

*Canker sores are also known as cold sores or herpes simplex (the oral variety). It is a common problem that is annoying, inconvenient and painful. There are no cures at this time, but we can speed the healing process and give you some comfort with this great little recipe. If you want to skip the beeswax (helps hold the ingredients on the wound) here's some other choices:*

*Mix the "active ingredients," minus the beeswax, into melted petroleum jelly.*

*Omit the beeswax or petroleum jelly and just make up the "active ingredients" as a mix and apply to the canker sore. You may re-apply every two hours for relief.*

1½ tablespoons (23ml) melted beeswax (or petroleum jelly)
1 teaspoon (5ml) sweet oil
5 drops camphor
1,000 to 1,800 IU vitamin C tablet crushed (or vitamin C powder)

Melt the beeswax. As it cools, add the sweet oil, camphor and vitamin C powder. Stir until cool enough to apply. Store in a bottle with name and make date.

Shelf Life: Approx. 4 days to 1 week — Keep in the refrigerator.

# NERVES

Kava Kava is a root that induces physical and mental relaxation and is helpful for anxiety and stress-related disorders. There is no special formula here; just look in your health food store for capsules and follow the directions. Caution: Kava can cause some drowsiness, so do not operate cars or other machinery when using it.

Other remedies include: chamomile tea with a little milk and honey; although it's not as strong as the Kava, and other teas such as passionflower, chamomile and lemon balm. Best of all, take some time out of your day to relax in a hot bath, sniff some lavender and rose essential oils and light a candle. Create an ambience to soothe away the troubles of the day.

# INSOMNIA

Valerian root and passionflower are two of the most powerful herbs to promote sleep. Chamomile is also a relaxant. You can make a tea from any of these herbs, or take them as tinctures. Melatonin is also a great sleep inducer. You can buy melatonin in tablet form and tinctures at your local health food supplier.

# MOTION SICKNESS

Ginger has long been used by the Asian community to calm upset tummies. There are also acupressure points that work well. Here are some things that will help.

- Make concentrated ginger tea and drink it slowly.

- Chew on candied ginger or ginger-flavored candies.

- Be still, keep your eyes on the horizon line and get fresh air.

- A mild peppermint tea helps calm upset tummies, especially in kids (make the tea very weak for kids).

You also can buy drug-free wrist bands that have a knob which you place on a spot of your wrist. It really helps with motion sickness, or you can apply pressure to that spot yourself. The spot is to the inside of your wrist, just about ½" to ¾" (13mm to 19mm) below the base of your thumb.

# ITCHING AND RASHES

## Poison Oak and Poison Ivy Relief

*Make this recipe and spread on the infected areas. Let it sit 15 minutes and then wash off. On the first day, if needed, it can be applied every couple of hours for additional relief.*

¼ cup (57g) lightly cooked rolled oats
¼ cup (18g) powdered milk
1 tablespoon (21g) honey
1 tablespoon (29g) aloe vera gel

Mix this all together into a paste. If it is too thick, add water to make a smooth texture. Place in container labeled with name and make date.

Shelf Life: 3 to 4 days — Keep in the refrigerator.

# TEETHING

Babies want to rub or have rubbed the area where the tooth is coming in because it hurts. A mild passionflower tea will help a fretful child while giving him a rubber teething ring to suck on. I also have seen several numbing products made with alcohol. Numbing the area is effective, and while I do not suggest feeding your baby alcohol, a little vodka on a clean finger or cotton swab rubbed on the gums often will provide some relief.

## Sweet Passionflower Popsicle

*My favorite, however, is to make a passionflower Popsicle. Let the child suck on it or rub on the sore area to make it numb.*

**Prepared passionflower tea (mild)**
**A little sweetener or natural fruit juice of your choice**

Freeze on a Popsicle stick.

# HICCUPS

I learned this remedy from a doctor when I worked in an emergency room. It works, and it is amazing, but you've got to find the "right spot" for it to work. You cannot do this to yourself, as it is too hard to find the right spot and apply pressure on yourself. This poor patient came into emergency because he had been hiccuping for a whole day. The hiccups had become so violent that it was causing him to be sick (an extreme case to be sure). I watched the doctor perform this technique and in three minutes the patient was smiling and better. Well, I just had to learn to do this, and each time I apply it, I am still amazed.

Using the outside of your thumb, press slightly above the collarbone just to the outside of the dip in the throat. While applying firm pressure (in and downward), ask the person to slowly take big deep breaths of air, in and out, and concentrate on the breathing. You must be careful when you do this, you do not want to block the airway or the person will choke. If the person struggles a little to cough, you are too close to the airway. Move your thumb slightly outward toward their shoulder, but not much; you want to be as close to the airway as possible without making the person feel like you are blocking it. Do not apply the pressure for more than 60 seconds at a time. This procedure usually controls the hiccups in one to three minutes. You may need a second try, but if done right the method really works. It works because the nerves along the carotid artery that "allow" you to hiccup are temporarily blocked while this procedure is performed and the person is breathing slowly.

# SCARRING

Vitamin E can be used as a topical application or taken internally in capsule form to prevent scarring. To use externally, prick open one end of a 1,000 IU capsule (sometimes you can find vitamin E in liquid form) and apply the oil directly to the injured area before scars have fully formed, or take the vitamin E as a capsule, per the instructions on the bottle.

## Stretch Mark Oil

*It is so important to keep the skin moist and supple so the skin does what nature intended...stretch gracefully to accommodate the growth of life within. Apply every night to your stomach.*

**3 ounces (90ml) olive oil**
**3 ounces (90ml) jojoba oil**
**6 vitamin E capsules (or ½ teaspoon (2.5ml) liquid vitamin E)**

Pierce the vitamin E capsules and extract the liquid. Mix together with the olive and jojoba oil. Store in a bottle labeled with name and make date.

Shelf Life: 9 months

# HOT FLASHES

Along with simple cooling of your body, look for herb tea or supplement combinations offered with the following herbs to help with menopausal symptoms. The first three are the most effective, but the other ingredients help support the first three herb's effectiveness.

**Black cohash root**          **Motherwort**
**Chaste tree berry**          **Sage**
**Wild yam**                   **Blue vervain**
**Pomegranate**                **Ginseng**
**Green tea**                  **Soy**

# CHAPTER THREE

# CLEAN UP WITH SAVINGS AND SAVE THE ENVIRONMENT

# AROUND THE HOME

With the high cost of cleaning products and worry about chemicals being introduced into your home environment, it's not surprising you want the knowledge to take control. In this chapter, I am going to show you how to make your own products from scratch and give you simple ideas that take very little effort. Simpler is better when it comes to cleaning products, and safe and gentle products will work.

I also include heavy-duty products that you can make with nothing but a disinfecting ingredient. Depending on your needs, you get the power to control the strength of the product, thereby controlling your costs as well.

Some of the general cleaners can be used several places throughout the house. The shelf life of these products is very good, so you can make a large batch of a product to use whenever you need it. Keep all household cleaners out of the reach of children.

## KITCHEN AND BATH

Let's start with the hard-core cleaning first. The kitchen and bathroom are the areas in your home where you worry most about germs, bacteria and mold, and where the major water centers are located. For the following cleansers, wear gloves, keep out of the reach of children, and do not use on fabrics. Never mix bleach with ammonia — dangerous fumes can result. Do not leave disinfectants or cleaners in toilet bowls unattended if you have pets that are tempted to drink from the toilet.

All the following formulas have a four to six month shelf life unless otherwise noted.

# Gentle Oven Cleaner

2 ounces (60ml) vinegar
½ teaspoon (2.5ml) cinnamon essential oil (or citrus essential oil, such as orange or lemon)
¼ cup (56g) baking soda

Mix all ingredients into a paste. Use a scrub pad to clean the oven.

> Spot Cleaning the Oven
> Use straight essential oil of cinnamon, orange or lemon for spot cleaning your oven from tough baked-on grime. Add enough oil to allow the mixture to cover the grime spot for 15 to 20 minutes. Wash off with soapy water. The oils of cinnamon, orange and lemon will not only make your kitchen smell great, but they are also very caustic. Left on long enough, they will eat right through grime, grease and oil.

*The recipe will foam, so mix it in a large container to allow for the bubbling expansion. Use gloves to protect your hands. This does not store well, so mix it and use it.*

# Simple Drain Cleaner

2 ounces (60ml) ammonia
1 teaspoon (5ml) cinnamon essential oil (or one of the citrus oils)
½ cup (111g) baking soda
2 ounces (60ml) white vinegar

Mix all ingredients together to make a paste. For clog, pour paste down the drain and let sit for 30 minutes. Run water down drain to flush. For burnt-on foods, use a heavy-duty sponge and scrub racks with the paste. When finished, mist with water and wipe clean. This mixture will not store well. Make and use immediately

*Along with cleaning the drain, this more caustic formula also works great for cleaning those stubborn "burnt on spots" on your oven rack and the racks of your barbecue grill. Use a large container, as this recipe will bubble and expand. The mixture of ammonia and cinnamon/citrus oils are caustic and will eat through and dissolve the clog. The baking soda and vinegar clean and sanitize the drain. Wear gloves to protect your hands.*

# Toilet, Tile and Tub Cleaner

4 ounces (120ml) water
2 ounces (60ml) ammonia
2 ounces (60ml) white vinegar
1 tablespoon (14g) baking soda

Mix the ingredients together and keep in a glass container. Store in a cool, dry place and keep out of the reach of children. Label the container with name and make date.

Shelf Life: 8 months to 1 year

*Use rubber gloves when working with ammonia.*

**$ COST COMPARISON**
**Homemade: $1.29 for 24 ounces**
**Soft Scrub™: $4.50 for 23 ounces**

## Countertop Cleaner

*I like to put this cleaner in a spray bottle (recycled plastic) and keep it under my sink. If I have a stain on a plastic surface, I mix a few drops of peroxide into ¼ cup (60ml) of this homemade cleanser. If you want a stronger recipe, add three tablespoons (45ml) isopropyl alcohol to the cleaning mixture.*

**3 tablespoons (45ml) liquid Castile soap, store-bought or homemade, page 50**
**½ teaspoon (3g) borax**
**1 teaspoon (5g) baking soda**
**1½ cups (360ml) water**
**4 ounces (120ml) witch hazel**
**5 drops tea tree extract or oil**
**5 drops orange oil or lemon oil**

Dissolve the tea tree and citrus oils into the witch hazel. Blend in all the remaining ingredients. Store in a bottle labeled with name and make date. Shake before using.

Shelf Life: 3 to 6 months

If you don't want to make the liquid Castile soap (page 50), you can purchase it from your local store.

"Washing soda" (sodium carbonate), also known as soda ash, is a naturally occurring mineral found in sea beds. Sometimes, it is used in soaps and other cleaning compounds, as well as antacids. A little bit of soap flakes (another basic soap that contains soda ash) can be reconstituted in water to make a great cleaning solution for your laundry, dishes and basic cleaning needs (as does liquid Castile soap). Make this for a fraction of the cost of many store-bought alternatives.

## Toilet Bowl Disinfectant or Tile Mold Treatment

*Use this solution to clean the toilet bowl. To use as a sanitizer, bleaching agent and mold killer on tile and grout, cut the water in this recipe to ½ cup (120ml). Place it on the mold spots formed on tile or grout.*

**1½ cups (360ml) water**
**1 tablespoon (15ml) lemon juice**
**4 ounces (120ml) liquid bleach**
**⅛ teaspoon (.5ml) liquid bluing (sometimes called liquid whiting — this is a bleach)**

Wear gloves to protect your hands from the bleach and bluing. Mix all ingredients together. Store in a container labeled with name and make date.

Shelf Life: 6 months

# IN THE LAUNDRY

## Gentle Laundry Detergent

**1 cup (221g) baking soda**
**½ cup (114g) cup borax**
**1 cup (227g) clear glycerin soap flakes from glycerin bar soap**

Grate clear glycerin soap into small flakes (as small as possible). In a large glass bowl, mix the soap flakes, baking soda and borax. Store as a liquid mixture. If you cannot get the soap flakes small enough, put gloves on and make ready-to-go washing-machine balls. Mix the ingredients together, mashing them into single-use balls about one-half inch (13mm) in diameter. When it's time to do laundry, put in your clothes and pop in a "laundry ball." Keep in a sealed container labeled with name and make date.

Shelf Life: 1 to 2 months supply

Some stores sell old-fashioned "washing soda." You can buy this multi-purpose washing powder (it is a concentrate) for a fraction of the price of commercial brands. Follow the directions for use.

# Hard Water Low-Cost Fabric Softener for the Washer

**¼ cup (57g) borax**
**Purchased laundry detergent (per directions)**

Shelf Life: 12 months

*Borax is inexpensive, just add about ¼ cup (57g) for each load of laundry along with your regular detergent if you have hard water. You do not need to add borax if you are using the homemade laundry detergent; it's already in the mix.*

# Gentle Pre-Treating Spray

**4 ounces (120ml) white vinegar**
**½ cup (110g) baking soda**
**8 ounces (240ml) water**

Mix all ingredients together and pour into a spray bottle. Label with name and make date.

Shelf Life: 2 months

*Put this recipe in a handy spritz bottle and use to pre-treat spots on your clothes before adding to the washer.*

## Reusable Dryer Fabric-Softener Bags

*You can double or triple this recipe and you'll have plenty on hand for a long time.*

**¼ cup (55g) baking soda**
**2 teaspoons (5g) cornstarch**
**3 drops of your favorite essential oil**

Make a refillable bag out of a sheer piece of fabric. Sift the dry ingredients. Add the fragrance and sift two to three more times to infuse the dry ingredients. Put about one tablespoon (15g) of the mix into the fabric bag and gather the top with a rubber band. Toss in the dryer.

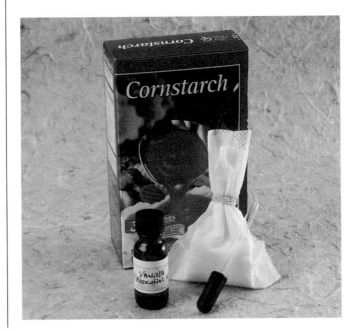

## Natural Spray Starch

*Adapted from an old recipe used by Victorian ladies to stiffen doilies for Christmas tree ornaments, this simple starch recipe is easy to make and doesn't cost much. Make a stiffer spray by adding more cornstarch or make a very gentle starch by adding more water. Cornstarch easily washes out, so there won't be any build-up on your shirts.*

*For removing specific stains, see the information for removing stains from carpets on page 126. The techniques also work on fabric.*

**2 tablespoons (16g) cornstarch**
**2 cups (480ml) warm water**

Shelf Life: 2 to 3 months

# FLOOR TO CEILING SOLUTIONS

If you want someone to "change the subject," just start talking about cleaning. Yet, we need to clean and we want it to be effective, safe, quick and affordable. Use the following recipes for your cleaning regime and feel happier, healthier and a little more "green."

Most of the time you won't need to go to this extreme, as simple occasional dusting will do. However, there are times when you need to wash things down. For example, you just bought a house and the previous owners did a lot of frying in the kitchen and the walls look a bit dingy. There's grease build-up on the walls and then dust has stuck to that. It may be a fine layer, but it would dull the paint. Or, you've just added onto your home and put up new sheet rock — dust is everywhere and you need to clean up the fine dust from your walls and ceilings.

Before you begin, make sure the walls are washable. Do not use these cleaners on wallpapered surfaces or flat paint. It's better to dry-dust those types of walls.

To clean ceilings and walls, use the all-purpose cleaner, but make it easy on yourself and use a paint roller and sponge mop. First, make sure you protect the floors from drips. A bunched-up towel on the handle will also catch any drips coming down from the handle. Put a thin coat of the cleaner on the roller — just roll it on. Afterward, use your sponge mop to go over the area and remove the cleaner and the dirt. The long handles will make this job easier.

> Remove floor scuffs and marks off of painted walls with an art gum eraser.

# CLEAN AND POLISH

Safe for the environment and safe for you and your family, this all-in-one, handy-dandy home cleaning recipe will be used over and over again. It's a great basic cleaner that can be made in advance and it tackles many jobs. The liquid Castile, baking soda and vinegar are the workhorses and the tea tree extract and witch hazel are light antiseptics providing grease-cutting and antibacterial properties without leaving a residue. If you like, add a few drops of your favorite essential oil to create your "clean" smell.

## All-Purpose Cleaner

**2 ounces (120ml) water**
**½ cup (110g) baking soda**
**4 ounces (120ml) liquid Castile (or 4 ounces homemade glycerin soap cleanser below)**
**1 teaspoon (5ml) tea tree extract or tincture**
**2 ounces (30ml) witch hazel**

Mix all the ingredients together. Pour into a spray bottle. Keep in a cool place. Label the bottle with name and make date.

Shelf Life: 6 months

## Homemade Glycerin Soap Cleanser

Here's an alternative for the liquid Castile in the All-Purpose Cleaner recipe if you cannot find liquid Castile, or it is too expensive in your area. Purchase a four-ounce (112g) glycerin soap bar. Melt it on the stove top over low heat. Do not let it boil. When melted, stir in an equal amount of water and stir until cool. Place in a bottle labeled with name and make date.

Shelf Life: 12 months

# Heavy-Duty Window Cleaner

*A heavy-duty window cleaner for tough jobs.*

**2 ounces (60ml) isopropyl alcohol**
**2 ounces (60ml) white vinegar**
**¼ teaspoon (1g) baking soda**
**1 tablespoon (30ml) liquid Castile or glycerin soap cleanser, page 122**
**3 cups (720ml) water**

Mix the ingredients together. Store in a container labeled with name and make date.

Shelf Life: 6 months

# Non-Alcohol Window Cleaner

*A mild window cleaner, but on "normally dirty" windows it works fine.*

**4 ounces (120ml) white vinegar**
**¼ teaspoon (1g) baking soda**
**1 tablespoon (30ml) liquid Castile or glycerin soap cleanser, page 122**
**3 cups (720ml) water**

Mix all ingredients together. Pour into a recycled spray bottle. Label with name and make date.

Shelf Life: 6 months

$ **COST COMPARISON**
**Homemade: $0.45 for 26 ounces**
**Windex™: $3.99 for 26 ounces**

## Wood Furniture Polish

*Easy-to-make recipe works as good as other cleaners on the market that wipe away dirt and protect wood finishes. This also can be used to revive tired-looking wood floors.*

**4 ounces (120ml) walnut oil (can substitute olive or sunflower oil, but walnut is best)**

**1 tablespoon (15ml) melted beeswax, from bar**

**1 teaspoon (5ml) linseed oil**

**1 to 2 drops citrus essential oil**

Cut off a portion of the beeswax bar to make one tablespoon (15ml) of melted wax. Pour melted beeswax into the other oils. Mix well. Store in a container or spray bottle. Label with name and make date.

Shelf Life: 6 months

## Gentle Wood Cleaner

*Remove dust and add shine with this wood furniture cleaner. The oils are a little more expensive, but slightly better. The lecithin helps emulsify the oil and soap together.*

**2 ounces (60ml) canola cooking oil or olive oil**

**3 tablespoons (45ml) liquid Castile soap (store-bought or homemade, page 50)**

**1 teaspoon (2g) lecithin**

Add the ingredients together and stir for three to five minutes. Store in a container labeled with name and make date. Shake before using.

Shelf Life: 3 to 4 months

If you find an old piece of furniture that needs refinishing, but you love the design, restore it. There are a lot of great books about refinishing to help you complete the job. This nifty little recipe helps loosen the old cracked paint or stain prior to scraping. There is acetone in the recipe, but it's still gentler than some of the commercial brands. The mix is caustic and strong enough to eat through the wood, so do not leave it on the wood for more than 20 minutes. For heavily painted surfaces, use a paint scraper or razor blade in a holder and do not dig at the piece; it will damage the wood. Use a light, vertical motion. If the paint was lightly applied and it comes up easily, use a stainless steel scrub pad. Place the removed paint on newspaper and dispose of properly. This remover should be used only on painted parts. It will work as a solvent on virgin wood and cause damage. Wear gloves and work in a well-ventilated area. Remember, keep it away from pets and kids.

# Paint Remover

**4 ounces ( 120ml) benzoil**
**2 ounces (60ml) isopropyl alcohol**
**2 ounces (60ml) acetone**
**1 teaspoon (5ml) melted beeswax**

Melt the beeswax. Add the rest of the ingredients and mix well. Label the container with name and make date. Store in a safe place.

Shelf Life: Approx. 18 months

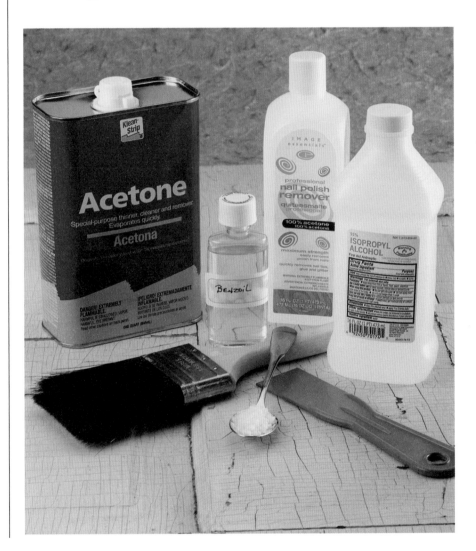

# CARPET CURES

*For new, liquid spills standing on top of the carpet or upholstered furniture, toss on this powder. Let sit for a minute, then sweep or vacuum the area. To lift old dried-on stains, add just enough water to make a paste, then apply to the surface and let sit for approximately 30 minutes. Brush off with a stiff-bristled brush and vacuum the surface, if necessary.*

*These natural solutions will help you remove unwanted products and stains from your carpets.*

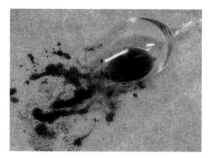

## Dry Carpet Cleaner and Deodorizer

¼ cup (114g) baking powder
¼ cup (32g) cornstarch
⅛ cup (32g) arrowroot powder

Sift the baking powder, cornstarch and arrowroot powder together. Store in a cheese shaker. Label with name and make date.

Shelf Life: 12 months

## Gum and Wax

Place ice on gum or wax to harden. Peel it off. Put a scrap piece of porous non-colored paper over the remains. Place a hot iron on top of the paper to transfer remains of the gum or wax from the fabric to the paper. You may need to repeat a few times with clean paper (a brown paper grocery bag works well). If remnants from the gum or wax are still visible, use a pre-treating spray soak. Finish cleaning with cold soapy water.

## Grease and Oil

First, use Dry Carpet Cleaner (see recipe above) to soak up excess oil. Then, mix ½ cup (120ml) hot soapy water with one teaspoon (5ml) glycerin to clean and remove stain. For tougher stains, try ¼ cup (60ml) glycerin mixed with three tablespoons (45ml) turpentine. Test a small spot for colorfastness before applying to entire area.

## Ink

Use cream of tarter to soak up the ink and follow with a cold water wash. Apply Dry Carpet Cleaner (see recipe above).

## Blood, Red Wine, Tomato and Chocolate

Make a paste of one teaspoon (5g) borax, one tablespoon (14g) baking soda and enough cold water to make a paste. Lightly scrub the stain and let the paste sit for approximately 10 minutes. Rinse with cold water and let dry. Repeat if necessary. Follow with Dry Carpet Cleaner (see recipe above).

Enzyme-type produ...  available
at your pet supply stores . you don't
have any homemade on hand. Apply
as directed as soon as possible.

## "Oops," Pet Stain Remover

Make your own enzyme-type, pet stain remover. Catch the potty spot right away and add a small amount of 50 percent club soda and 50 percent white vinegar to the spot. Soak up as much as you can with paper towel. Repeat. This will cut the urine smell and help lift the stain into the paper towel. Repeat a few times, but do not oversaturate the area (apply small amount, soak up completely, apply small amount again, soak up completely). It's a good idea to keep a filled spray bottle handy for fast application if you have a puppy or incontinent animal.

## Pet Smell Carpet Cures

When I was designing product formulas, I was approached by a group of realtors, who asked if there was any product I could develop to cut the pet smell in carpeting. Some of their property listings had good carpeting, but lingering pet smells made the home unattractive to buyers and sometimes, it held up the sale of the property.

Animal urine is one of the most challenging smells to get out of flooring. Carpet is the worst because urine travels down through the carpet to the padding and flooring below. There are two basic ways to approach this problem when the smell is strong: on the surface of the carpet or down into the pad and the sub-floor under the carpet. Most people treat the carpet surface which makes the carpet look better, but the smell stays because they cannot get to the odors below without ripping up the carpet.

Strong essential oils, such as vanilla and pineapple, do a good job of neutralizing pet odors. You'll want to address each of the carpet layers and here's how you do it. It is effective in most cases.

You need to work from the bottom up. Essential or strong fragrance oil concentrates may leave marks on the carpet so do not pour this on the surface of the carpet. You want to get past the carpet into the pad and sub-floor. What better way to inject the solution than to use a hypodermic syringe with all the working parts minus the needle?

Draw the straight fragrance or oil up into the syringe. Using your fingers, part the fibers of the carpet until you can see the base. Inject a drop or two just into the base of the pad. Repeat this process in various parts of the carpet where you think the smell is strongest, approximately every six inches (15cm). There will be certain areas where the pet went, as they are creatures of habit. Let this sit for a few hours, then come back and lightly sprinkle baking soda on the carpet top in those same areas. Let it sit overnight and then vacuum. If it is a light to medium odor, this probably will fix the problem. If the odor was strong, you may have to repeat. Let your nose be your guide. This solution is for carpet only. You easily can wash or scrub other floors when there is no "hidden" area like the carpet padding, and usually, that is where the carpet odor is lurking.

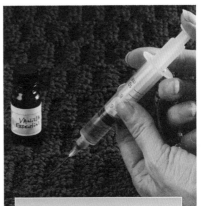

This solution also works on the smell of smoke from smokers. Of the two scents, vanilla is the easiest to find. Baking soda also is a good odor eliminator.

# PRECIOUS METAL CLEANERS

## Silver Cleaner

*You have to be careful with silver. For many, it is their pride and joy on display. Use a soft cloth to apply a small amount of the cleaner to the item and gently rub. Use a soft toothbrush to get at hard-to-reach places. Do not scrub hard — silver scratches. When finished, buff with a clean cloth. Make as much of this cleaner as you need for one time. It does not store well.*

Store your silver with little silica bags to retard moisture which causes silver to tarnish.

**Equal parts baking soda and club soda**

Dissolve the baking soda into the club soda. Make a paste. Use immediately.

## Copper Cleaner

*Copper also is a soft metal, so again, be careful not to scrub too hard. Clean often to avoid that "black" look from copper tarnish. Apply cleaner to the item and rub until clean. Rinse off cleaner with water and shine with a clean, soft cloth.*

**2 tablespoons (29g) tomato ketchup**
**¼ teaspoon (1.5ml) lemon juice**

Mix together into a paste. Use immediately.

## Gold Cleaner

*Gold is a soft metal (carat gold or gold plated). Gold-plated is a metal or glass with a gold covering which adds strength. Lightly rub the gold with a soft cloth — do not scrub.*

**2 ounces (60ml) liquid Castile soap (store-bought or homemade, page 50)**
**⅛ teaspoon (.7ml) ammonia**
**2 ounces (60ml) water**

Mix together and store in a glass bottle. Label with name and make date.

Shelf Life: 4 to 6 months

# THE GARAGE AND EXTERIOR OF YOUR HOME

In the garage and around your home, considerable amounts of useless and unwanted chemicals can pile up. It might be time to take inventory of all your old chemical items lurking in the garage and in your "cleaning supply" cabinet.

If you have commercial household chemicals older than two years, you may want to consider getting rid of them. Many of them can become concentrated over time; some of the solvents evaporate into the air, your home and garage. When they become dry and not suitable for use, why keep them around? They are taking up unnecessary space, creating clutter and possibly becoming a fire hazard.

Look around your garage and in your cupboards and garden sheds. Round up any and all unused chemicals, including: herbicides, pesticides, commercial fertilizers, used motor

oil, old paint and thinner, and any other old chemical substances. Have a chemical clean-up day! Be sure and dispose of these items properly and safely. A couple of times a year, most recycling centers have a special day for proper disposal of these items without a charge. Never pour these products down the drain or put them in the regular trash! You could create a hazard for people, pets or the environment.

When it comes to handling all these chemicals, you need to arm yourself with tools, such as those listed below, for personal protection.
Heavy gloves
A paint mask to lessen the effects of inhalants
Full clothing to protect your skin
Sensible shoes (not sandals)
Safety glasses

- Suit up with proper clothing. Take one box at a time and collect all old commercial chemicals to be sorted later. Make sure lids are tight or securely capped to avoid mixing them or splashing them on yourself.

- Assemble all chemicals in a well-ventilated area on an old (or covered) table and start sorting.

- Sort all the chemicals you believe to be more than two years old. Any recent purchases should be labeled with your best guess of the purchase date. When you buy chemicals in the future, use an inexpensive white label and put the date of purchase on the outside.

- Continue sorting all chemicals until you have three sets of labeled boxes: Garden, Household and Garage. Prepare the old chemicals for disposal at the recycling center. Have items identified so the recycling center processes them correctly. Make sure you transport the chemicals you are discarding in a trunk or pickup truck. Keep away from yourself and other people.

- Store all of the chemicals you are keeping and in a cool, dry place — out of the reach of children and pets. Do not put chemicals in plastic bags. The bags may break and cause a hazard or melt the plastic and cause extra fumes (possibly dangerous).

- Do not smoke or stand near heaters or electrical equipment during this process.

# CAR, BOAT AND RV CLEANERS

For me and my family, these items represent having fun, so it's hard to think about cleaning them. However, when I go to the store and stroll the aisle of specialty products designed to clean, shine and protect my "investment," even I feel overwhelmed by the amount of different brands, prices and promises offered by the manufacturers. They all claim to do the same things. Then, there is the expensive chamois you can buy to make your cleaned item shine. Do you know that a bag of cloth diapers works just as well? You can have one for your car, one for your furniture polish, one for your windows, etc., and you can wash them and re-use for as long as they last. I'm getting all wound up about this, so let's get started!

## Car and Boat Cleaner

*Let's start with a basic soap for cleaning your car or boat. Add glycerin to boost the liquid soap strength, baking soda for extra cleaning and isopropyl alcohol for a clean with no residue.*

**4 cups (960ml) basic liquid soap, page 122**
**2 tablespoons (30ml) glycerin**
**2 ounces (60ml) isopropyl alcohol**
**⅛ cup (29g) baking soda**

Mix all ingredients together. Store in a container labeled with name and make date.

Shelf Life: 4 months

To remove tar, pitch or other sticky residue on your car or boat, use cooking oil. Rub the oil onto the sticky material (be generous) then allow it to soften. Carefully, scrape off the sticky material. If it's cold outside, it will help the process if you first warm the cooking oil.

## Car and Boat Wax

*Apply as you would any paste wax. Buff well and you'll have a beautiful shine!*

**1 cup (227g) carnauba wax**
**¾ cup (174g) beeswax**
**¼ cup (60ml) canola oil**

Melt the beeswax and carnauba wax together over low heat. Remember, wax is flammable at high temperatures so be patient. When melted, stir in oil. Pour into a glass or tin container and let harden. Label with name and make date.

Shelf Life: 1 year

## Tire Cleaner

*Brush this solution onto tires and sidewalls to help whiten. Wash again with the cleaning solution above.*

**2 cups (480ml) Car and Boat Cleaner (recipe above)**
**1 cup (442g) baking soda**

Mix the ingredients together. Make and use immediately.

Alternative modes of transportation like bicycles, mopeds, scooters, etc., will save you money and help save the environment by consuming less gas. The cleaning compounds also work on these types of vehicles.

*Clean leather furniture or car seats with just a small amount of this cleaner (works on vinyl too). Some leathers are better quality then others so be sure to check for colorfastness on any leather. Follow by moisturizing with a natural oil such as olive oil, sweet almond oil or canola oil. A lot of cowboys use straight glycerin soap for "saddle soap" as it usually costs less.*

*Brrrrrr. It's cold outside and everything is frozen. I don't want to spend a lot of time outside scraping my windshield. When we were younger, my husband, Byron, went with me to the store. He was reaching for some spray to de-ice the windshield. Of course, I grabbed the bottle (no ingredients) and stood there pondering a minute; he just sighed and put it back on the shelf. Well, I felt bad knowing that my family gets frustrated because I need to try and figure out formulas (so true…). I did some research on a Web site for chemicals to see what ingredients were in the deicer. Then, I bought some ingredients and proudly presented Byron with a bottle of my own deicer formula. He indulgently smiled, tried it, and told me later that it really did work as well as his commercial brand. (Behind my back — the nerve!)*

*Most deicers have propylene glycol. Both propylene glycol and alcohol usually don't freeze at the temperatures we have in the winter and both ingredients are water soluble. The water in the recipe helps the deicer glide on and soften the ice so the two other ingredients can penetrate and break up the ice so it slides off. It also prevents the mixture from being too strong on the paint.*

*This deicer is inexpensive and very similar to the commercially sold deicers. If you cannot find propylene glycol, substitute the same amount of a commercial antifreeze in the recipe. Many antifreeze formulas contain a high percentage of propylene glycol.*

## Leather Cleaner

**⅛ cup (30ml) isopropyl alcohol**
**1½ cups (360ml) water**

Mix ingredients together. Store in a container labeled with name and make date.

Shelf Life: 2 to 4 months

## Windshield Deicer

**¾ cup (180ml) propylene glycol**
**1 quart (960ml) water**
**3 cups (720ml) isopropyl alcohol**

You can play with the proportions I have given you, but keep in mind the lessons listed at left. Mix all the ingredients together. Store in a glass or heavy plastic container. Store in a cool dry place. Label with name and make date.
Keep this out of the reach of children and pets.

Shelf Life: 12 months

### IN-A-PINCH ANTIFREEZE

Depending on the size of your gas tank, add one to two cups (240ml to 480ml) isopropyl alcohol. The alcohol works as a solvent and helps keep the gas from freezing in your tank. Repeat every two to three weeks for stored vehicles that contain gas.

Most starting fluids are ethyl alcohol (grain alcohol). If your car won't start, spray a little ethyl alcohol into the air intake valve on the carburetor; try again to start your car.

# COST-SAVING CAR TIPS

Cars are an integral part of life for most of us. They not only transport us, but for some, they symbolize who we are. Some cars are sporty, some functional, and others luxurious, but whatever they are, they also are expensive.

Here are some cost-saving car tips my husband, Byron, and I want to pass on to you to help you save money.

- Have your car running at peak efficiency.

- Maximize your time in the car so you do not waste precious (and expensive) fuel.

- The heavier your car, the more it costs to run. Consider buying a lighter, fuel-efficient vehicle.

- Use cruise control on long trips to save money.

- Do not "rev" your engine at stop signs, when starting the engine or before shutting it off. These acts cause you to burn more gas and they increase wear on the engine.

- Carpool, take your bike, use the bus or another form of mass transit.

- Travel when the rest of the "crowd" is not — early mornings or late evenings.

- Quicker transit time equals gas savings. Idling in long traffic delays costs money.

- When possible, roll down the windows for cooling the car. The heater and the air conditioner lower the miles per gallon of gas for your car.

- You easily can get 15 percent more miles per gallon if you take care of your engine. Make sure you get regular tune-ups.

- Maintain your automobile yourself to save money.

- Change dirty oil. Dirty oil causes lower performance.

- Check the fan belt. If it is too tight, your engine is working too hard and it's not fuel-efficient.

- Snow tires use more gas. They are important to your safety, but remember to take them off your car when you no longer need them.

- Check spark plugs. Clean or replace when needed.

- Plan your trips. Make a list of everything you need before you go shopping. Do not waste precious time and gas making multiple trips to the store.

Baking soda neutralizes the corrosion on battery posts and cables. Apply a water and baking soda paste and let sit for one to three hours (depends on the corrosion). Repeat if needed. Wipe off posts and cables with disposable paper towel or cloth rag.

# ROOF, DECK AND CONCRETE CLEANERS

*If you are in the desert, this probably won't apply to you, but if you are in the rust belt...well, moss happens. There are a few things that moss doesn't like, from the least to the most toxic, here are things that will kill moss: vinegar, borax, trisodium phosphate and chlorine bleach.*

*This recipe can be used on your roof and some sidings. Use a long-handled brush to apply. Let sit for a few minutes, then rinse off. This is strong enough to pose a threat to some plants living under the rinse area so be aware of this and cover plants with plastic, if needed. This is a lot of work, so I have provided a quick shortcut below.*

*For cleaning your deck, use a vinegar, borax and water mix (⅓ each). Test a spot before applying to the whole deck.*

*For your roof, it usually takes a concentrate that is stronger. Use the recipe at right. Wear gloves, protective clothing and eyewear before making this recipe.*

## Roof and Deck Moss Remover

**1 gallon (4L) water**
**3½ cups (860ml) chlorine bleach**
**½ cup (116g) trisodium phosphate**

 Keep out of the reach of children and animals. These are toxic chemicals. Make and use immediately.

As an alternative moss remover, sprinkle Tide™ laundry detergent on your roof and leave on for eight to 24 hours. Hose off with a power washer. A lot of laundry powders have trisodium phosphate in them, so if you want to try another brand it's OK. Do not use a phosphate-free laundry powder, it may not work.

## Concrete Bleach

The Concrete Bleach recipe contains a couple of bleaches, so make sure you wear gloves and cover the surrounding mixing area. Scrub this mixture onto the stained area and let sit overnight. Hose off in the morning. Keep children and pets away until the area is rinsed the next day.

2 ounces (60ml) liquid cleaner such as All-Purpose Cleaner, page 122

2 tablespoons (30ml) chlorine bleach

2 cups (480ml) water

1 tablespoon (15ml) liquid whiting (sometimes called liquid bluing)

Mix all ingredients together. Store in glass container. Must be stored in a cool, dry place. Label container with name and make date.

 Keep out of the reach of children and animals.

Shelf Life: 2 to 3 months

## Garage Floor Spot Cleaner

Place cleaner on the grease spot. Let sit for a minute. Use paper towel to soak up the grease and cleaner.

2 ounces (60ml) isopropyl alcohol

1 tablespoon (15ml) cinnamon oil (or lemon or orange citrus oil)

# HOME EMERGENCY SUPPLIES

Most of us have lived through some emergencies both for our country and personally, so it makes good sense to have an area tucked away with necessary items...just in case. My mom used to joke that if you're prepared, nothing ever seems to happen, but if you're not prepared, then you are tempting fate.

We used to live far out in the country where storms would land an occasional tree across a power line and block road access. I learned to have candles and non-perishable food around. It may not seem important now, but if and when you ever need these things, you will be very glad you were prepared.

Just as you purchase car and life insurance to protect yourself and your loved ones, you need a little household emergency kit as insurance too. It doesn't need to be expensive or take up a lot of space. Buy one item at a time for your supply stash every time you go shopping until you have everything you need.

Here is a list of basics everyone should have on hand for their first-aid kit.

- First-aid book (explains actual first-aid procedures for a range of injuries/events)
- Antibacterial spray
- Benedryl™
- Adhesive bandages
- First-aid ointment
- Ace bandages
- Scissors and tweezers
- Large gauze pads and tape
- Syrup of ipecac
- Eye wash
- Tea tree oil
- Witch hazel
- Betadine liquid
- Sweet oil
- Cold tablets

- Basic pain medication (over-the-counter)
- Cough syrup
- Anti-diarrhea medication
- Candles (at least a dozen various sizes)
- Matches
- One week's worth of canned or dried foods (no cooking required)
- Extra blankets
- Two to three flashlights and batteries
- Battery-operated radio
- Cash securely stashed in your home ($50 to $100)
- Full gas can (5 to 10 gallons)
- Water for one week (drinking water, water to make food, baby formula, wash dishes, etc.)

The list on the previous page is the bare minimum to handle a range of emergencies. If you have small babies, keep extra formula and diapers handy. Also, store a small supply of your prescription medications.

We tend to think that disasters, like storms, power outages, earthquakes or floods won't happen to us; I hope they don't but, if the worst happens, I want you to be prepared. Being prepared is cheap insurance; plus you will feel secure knowing that if something should happen you are prepared to help yourself, your family, and possibly others.

If you live in a rural area and have storms that can take out your power for a week or longer, you may want to consider adding the following items to your list.

- Personal generator and fuel

- Propane cooker (for outdoor use only) and a few small propane bottle refills

- Deck of cards

- Books you have not read

- A game or two (non-electronic) to amuse yourself until the power comes back on

Take into consideration what local hazards are near you, if any, and add any necessary items. You know your region best. As an example, when Mount St. Helens erupted in 1980, we had a day or two of heavy ash fallout from the mountain. Now, we store a few painters' masks just in case of a repeat disaster.

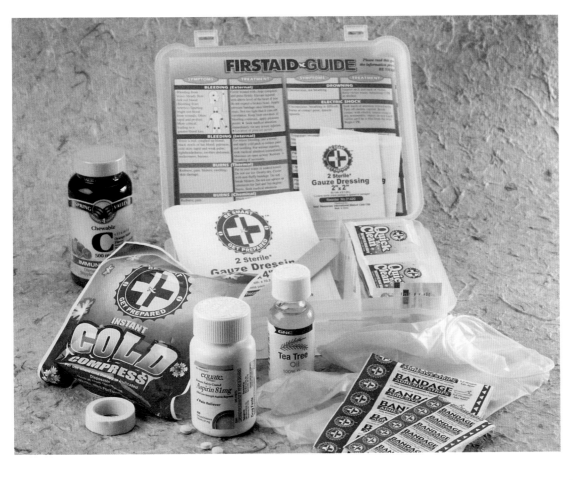

# HOME ENERGY FACTS

Recently, we've seen a huge surge in fuel and energy prices far above the standard rates for inflation. Now, everyone is concerned about spending less on home necessities. I asked my husband, Byron, who as a home builder is a handy guy to have around, to help me get back to the basics of an energy-efficient home.

Byron was raised on a farm and his parents were right out of the pages of "Mother Earth News." They had acreage, raised their own food, pinched pennies until it hurt, and recycled almost everything. They belonged to the "Grange," had timber in deferral, and belonged to county extension programs and the garden club. This is information we all can use to save money, and it's dedicated to my penny-pinching in-laws. They taught us a lot about saving energy way before it was trendy. Thanks Mom and Dad Kellar.

Let's start with standard energy use. According to several university studies, I've listed the ranges of power percentages used in households.

- Home heating: 56% to 58%

- Water Heating: 13% to 16%

- Refrigerator/Freezer: 4.6% to 9%

- Air Conditioning: 3% to 5%

- Cooking: 4% to 6%

- Lighting: 4% to 6%

- Television and Computers: 3% to 5%

- Clothes Drying: 1.5% to 2.5%

- Miscellaneous: 1% to 2.5%

Home heating and cooling represents 59 percent to 63 percent of the energy costs in the home, so this is where you can recoup the most savings.

Insulation will keep your home warm in the winter and cool in the summer. Insulation materials create a dead-air space that slows down the air transfer from outside to inside. To stay warm in the winter and decrease your home heating bill, you want to keep the cold air from getting in your house at its bottom. Stop drafts and provide good insulation in your floors and walls. To keep the warm air from escaping from the roof, install good ceiling insulation and circulation fans to move the heat downward. All these measures work the same way for hot weather too. When you use your air conditioner, the insulation traps the cold air inside and keeps the warm air out.

Some power companies will check your home and make suggestions for making it more energy efficient. Often, they will do this at no charge to you. Some companies even give energy or cash credits if you use this service because you are working cooperatively toward the same goal — less power usage through more efficient use of energy.

Insulating your home is an obvious start. When building, this is easy, but not so easy for some older homes. Check with a professional company that will give you an estimate for what you can afford and accomplish now.

# MONEY-SAVING ENERGY TIPS

- In the winter, create a barrier for a drafty door by rolling up a throw rug and placing it against the bottom of the door frame. Remember, cold seeks low points to enter the house.

- Close your blinds and curtains when it gets really cold at night to help keep heat inside. In the summertime, to help keep heat out, close them first thing in the morning before the temperature outside starts to rise.

- Turn down the thermostat in the winter when you go to bed and use grandma's comforter instead.

- During the day, dress warmer and lower your thermostat a few degrees to save money.

- Make sure your heat thermostat is clean and working correctly. Also, check to see if it is in a drafty location. This causes your furnace to work longer and overheat your home.

- If you have radiators, clean them regularly. If you have filters on your heat pump, clean the filters twice a year. Dirt can cover and block the flow of air around the radiator.

- Do not block heating or cooling vents with furniture or other items.

- If you have a large house and you're not using all the rooms, turn off the heat in the areas not used or close the doors to those rooms.

- Check to make sure all your vents to the house are insulated and functioning properly. Ceiling vents are critical, as they can lose a lot of heat from your house and increase your bill.

- Check the vent/damper in your fireplace. Close it when it is not in use.

- Wear warm socks and clothes in the winter. Watch television cuddled up under a blanket. You will feel warmer and you'll save money too.

- If you are in an area that cools down on summer evenings, turn off the air conditioner and open the windows.

- Use the exhaust fan in your kitchen to help warm air escape from your home when you are cooking in the summer.

- On hot days, make salads and barbecue outside so you don't add extra heat to the house.

- Clean your air conditioner and check the filter at the beginning of every season. If it is clogged, it will run longer than necessary. Make sure to clean the filter and/or replace it often.

- In the summertime or in warm climates, dress cool. My husband, Byron, is always too warm and I am always too cold. I love wearing sandals and being barefoot in the summer, but Byron will wear socks and tennis shoes and then complain he's too warm when I feel just right. I convinced him to start wearing shorts and sandals too. Now, I can turn down the air conditioner for both cost savings and my comfort. The moral of this story — dress according to the season or weather. A very simple and comfortable way to save money.

- Turn off the lights when you leave a room.

- Do not leave computers, televisions or radios running when you are not around.

- Use dimmer switches to lessen the wattage used at dinner and for other "marginal lighting" events.

- Eat by candlelight at least one night a week. Not only is it romantic, it will save you money. This is a great way to get a frugal guy into a romantic mood; tell him you're saving money.

- Switch to compact fluorescent lighting or LED lighting and only use a high-watt bulbs in areas where you need it, like a reading lamp or other critical areas.

- Instead of keeping a porch light on, use timers and motion sensors outside. They only come on when you need them.

- Put up light-colored (white or cream) shades on your lamp instead of dark shades which block light.

- Weatherproof windows and doors.

- Make doors and windows airtight. If you can see daylight around your doors or windows when they are closed, repairing them will save many energy dollars. It may be as easy as installing or repairing your weather stripping. Or, you may need to reset door hinges to get a better fit if they are seriously offset.

- Weather-stripping should last three to five years and it saves you a lot of money. There are several kinds of weather-stripping available, but the easiest is the adhesive-backed stripping. Make sure surfaces are clean and dry, pull off the tape backing and smoothly and evenly apply. Reinforce with small tacks spaced about every five inches (13cm).

- Install a door sweep on the bottom of the door. A sweep fits where the bottom of the door and the bottom door frame meet. For windows, and sometimes doors, use caulking to seal up cracks, then paint the caulking to match your door frame or walls.

- If you do not have storm windows, double-insulated windows or energy-efficient windows and you're on a budget, buy thick, clear plastic and make your own energy-efficient windows to cover the outside of the window. Tightly stretch the plastic over the window. Using a staple gun, staple the plastic to the window frame about every two to three inches (5cm to 8cm). This will create dead-air space insulation for your windows, and you still can see out the window.

# CHAPTER FOUR

# THE LOW-COST PAMPERED PET

Our pets provide so much more for us than we do for them. They can be a best friend, a form of therapy, a service animal, or just part of the family. Research tells us that they not only provide emotional support and companionship, but actually can slow our heart beat and lower our blood pressure when we spend loving, bonding time with them. They are ready to give love, easily forgive us and listen to our endless ramblings.

In a time where we need to carefully read ingredients in our food, we also need to look at what we are feeding our best friend. Some pet treats and foods contain unnecessary chemicals and fillers. Is this any way to treat your best friend?

Sometimes, the old techniques and remedies are still the best help for our animal buddies, but there are a lot of good, new ideas and trends, too. Many new products and services for pets are emerging: huge pet centers and stores, pet spas, pet cemeteries, pet day care, pet clothes, computer pets; I could go on and on. People are living longer, and after the kids grow up and leave home, pets sometimes find themselves in the roll of our kids. This section is dedicated to our pets. I have included products for helping pets with pests, pet treats and home remedies for your "pet kids." If you are like me, you may want to develop a new tradition and make special "new baby pet" treats to give to friends that acquire a new pet.

# HEALTHY DOG TREATS

Take a moment to whip up an easy-to-make pet treat for your pooch, cat or bird. When you make it yourself, you know they are getting fresh and nutritious treats.

## Buster's Peanut Butter Snack

1 cup (70g) crushed soda crackers
¾ cup (170g) ground oats
1 tablespoon (15g) soy powder
½ cup (120ml) bacon drippings
¼ cup (60ml) water
1 tablespoon (17g) peanut butter

Grind or crush the crackers to a fine powder. Melt the bacon drippings. Stir the peanut butter into the warm drippings. Add the ground crackers, oats and soy powder. Press this mixture into a pan. Bake at 325ºF (163ºC) for 15 to 20 minutes. When completely cooled, cut into squares or roll into balls. If your batch is too firm, add a little more bacon drippings and water the next time you make it. To make the batch firmer, add more ground crackers.

**$ COST COMPARISON**
**Homemade: $1.98 for 10**
**Jump One™ Treats: $5.25 for 10**

## Liver-Flavored Dog Biscuits

*Yummmm! Dogs love liver treats. The cats will eat this too — just make smaller bites.*

1½ cups (180g) whole-wheat flour

¼ cup (57g) powdered dry milk

¼ cup (60ml) water

1 egg

⅛ cup (30ml) vegetable oil

2 tablespoons (30g) unflavored yogurt

½ cup (113g) chopped liver

Mix all the ingredients together. Roll onto floured board (add more flour or water as needed). Make the biscuits about ½" (13mm) thick. Preheat oven to 300°F (149°C). Bake for 40 to 45 minutes. Slice when cool. Store in a container with lid. Label with name and make date.

Shelf Life: Approx. 2 months

## Popsicle Treat

When the weather is hot and uncomfortable, what kid does not enjoy a Popsicle to cool off? Here is a great idea to help cool off your pet. Your pet gets bored with the same old thing, just as we do. In hot weather, the water you give him quickly gets warm. We have a friend that bought two Popsicle-making trays, one for the kids and one for the dog. When the kids get a Popsicle, so does the dog. It is so cute to see him wiggle in expectation as the Popsicles are being handed out to the kids. He knows he'll get one in his special flavor too.

Dedicate one inexpensive ice cube tray to your pet. Add chicken- or beef-flavored soup stock, leftover meat drippings, or water drained from a can of tuna. Freeze in an ice-cube tray. Be inventive and think of more ideas, as long as it is safe and yummy.

In the evening, when you are sitting around having iced tea for dinner, pop a couple of frozen Popsicles into an old bowl and watch your pet cool off and have fun with a yummy treat.

## Healthy and Easy Pet Snacks

*Pets usually like plain Cheerios™ cereal, and it's a pet-safe "people food" that's a healthy alternative to other things you might be tempted to share. Make enough to use for a few days.*

**1 cup (30g) oat- or rice-based low-sugar cereal**
**3 tablespoons (45ml) meat juice (or water drained from a can of tuna)**

Remove excess fat from the meat juice. Drizzle meat juice or tuna water over the dry cereal. Too much fat is not good for you or your dog. Let dry. Pack in an airtight container. Label with name and make date.

## Good for People — Good for Pets

*Wouldn't you get bored eating the same old thing day after day? Make your pet's life more interesting and nutritious by giving them any of the cooked items, listed at right, once a week. These foods are good for you and good for your pet. Leave out gravies, sugars, butters, etc. This recipe will give your pet some variety in his diet, and since dogs and cats do not keep track of days, they'll always be surprised the day they get their treat.*

**Cooked chicken**
**Cooked brown rice**
**Cooked veggie mix (chopped up)**

### TIPS FOR THE FUSSY EATER

Whether it is your cat (more likely) or your dog, sometimes they get nervous or bored or don't feel well. Here are some ideas that may help get your pet back on track.

- Serve different brands/flavors of food at least three days a week.

- Remove any extraneous stimuli such as loud noises, kids, and other animals from the area when food is served.

- Try the health tonic on the next page to boost strength and appetite.

- Add a little onion powder (just a little) to make it more interesting. You also can put a small dab of peanut butter at the bottom of the dish. They will smell it and try to eat their way to it.

- If you always offer dry food, try a moist one, or vice versa.

## Pet Health Tonic
### (for dogs or cats)

*You want to see shiny coats, bright eyes and wet noses on your pet and this vitamin tonic will do the trick. Mix one teaspoon (5ml) of tonic each day in their food for added nutrients to their diet. The greens help stop the craving to eat grass and add vitamin A, the garlic detoxifies their systems, the oils give shine to their coats and add extra vitamins, and the brewer's yeast adds lots of healthy B vitamins to their diet. Do not exceed more than one teaspoon per day.*

¼ cup (60ml) cod liver oil
½ cup (120ml) water
½ cooked garlic clove
1 teaspoon (1.3g) fresh parsley
1 tablespoon (15ml) vegetable oil
¼ teaspoon (1g) brewer's yeast

Chop the cooked garlic clove and fresh parsley until very fine. Add the brewer's yeast. Mix in the remaining ingredients. Mix well. Keep in an amber bottle in the refrigerator. Shake well prior to each use. Label with name and make date.

Shelf Life: Approx. 2 months if kept in the refrigerator

# HEALTHY KITTY TREATS

## Kitty Tuna Treat

*Do you think your cat is finicky? Well, even the most finicky kitty will dive into this like a dog.*

*You can control the softness or firmness of this recipe by adding or taking away bread crumbs.*

Save the water from the tuna to make the fishy fertilizer on (page 167).

½ cup (120ml) chicken broth
2 ounces (60g) plain yogurt
7-ounce (1.2kg) can of tuna fish
1 to 2 slices of whole-wheat bread, crumbled

Put the broth into a small bowl. Add the bread crumbs and plain yogurt and stir until all the liquid is absorbed. Drain the water from the tuna. Add the tuna fish. Stir until smooth. If too soft, add a little more bread. Put in a sealed plastic container in the refrigerator for a few hours until firm. Cut into squares or roll into balls. Butter your hands when making the balls; it keeps the mix off your hands and cats like the taste of butter too.

## Here Kitty-Kitty Treats

*Train your kitty to come running when you call with this tasty treat. Control how moist or dry you want the treats by adding either more wheat flour or water.*

¼ cup (30g) whole-wheat flour

½ cup (114g) dry non-fat powdered milk

1 tablespoon (9g) cornmeal

1 raw egg, whipped

¼ cup (120ml) water

¼ cup (57g) powdered chicken stock

1 tablespoon (15ml) catnip

¼ cup (57g) cooked liver, finely chopped

Mix all ingredients together. Put in a plastic sealed container. Place in the refrigerator for a few hours. Knead the mixture, then shape into balls. Butter your hands so the mix doesn't stick to you. Label container with name and make date.

Shelf Life: Approx. 2 months

# PET BIRDS

*This recipe will appeal to a variety of birds. If you fry bacon save the grease, it adds flavor to the treat. Once you've prepared the treat, spread the mix onto small wood slabs and hang from a tree or roll into a shape or ball and put in your bird's cage.*

## High-Protein Bird Treats

1 cup (232g) solid bacon grease (or solid vegetable shortening)

1½ cups (162g) bread crumbs

1½ cups (300g) millet

¼ cup (36g) sunflower seeds

¼ cup (20g) rolled oats

½ cup (129g) peanut butter

Heat the bacon grease or shortening in a saucepan until softened. Remove from heat. In a separate bowl, combine the remainder of the ingredients and mix. Add the dry goods to the softened bacon grease or shortening, which should be partially set. Stir thoroughly.

# MINOR FIRST AID FOR PETS
## EAR CARE

### Ear Mites

*Wipe out your pet's ears with this recipe. It repels mites and keeps the ears fresh and clean. Following, wipe out the ears with oil from a vitamin E capsule to help promote healing.*

50/50 blend of apple-cider vinegar and water

Oil from a vitamin E capsule

### Yeast Infection in the Ears

*You can get yeast medications from your veterinarian, but my pet's groomer helped me save money with this suggestion. Put a small amount of the cream in your pet's ear using a cotton swab and rub into the ears.*

Human vaginal yeast infection cream (sold over the counter in most states)

Cotton swabs

# ITCHING AND RASHES

There are a few things that you can do to calm down irritated skin and itchy spots. First, make sure your pet is free of fleas and mites. This may require treating or changing their bedding area and perhaps treating your house and carpets, especially if it is an indoor pet.

*You can find colloidal oatmeal in most stores. It is used to calm the skin for humans and pets. Colloidal refers to the size of the oatmeal. It is fast-acting, very small and it's easy to use. You also can make your own similar product by grinding regular oatmeal in your food processor. If you purchase colloidal oatmeal use as is.*

*This process may be a bit messy. Gently cleanse the irritated area with the shampoo and leave on for 60 seconds. Then add oatmeal to calm down the irritation to give your pet some relief. After rinsing off the oatmeal and shampoo, apply a light non-scented lotion to the area. If it is an area they tend to bite or chew, prevent them from doing this by spraying on a light amount of bitter apple. (Bitter apple is a small lemon-size bitter fruit with a nasty taste.) A small amount of calamine lotion also works, but the wash is better. I recommend it for dogs because we all know how cats feel about water....There is a dry shampoo for cats and dogs on page 153.*

*The amount of shampoo you make will depend on the size of your animal. I have provided some suggestions. You can use one essential oil or make a combination of two or more oils to achieve the fragrance of your choice.*

## Colloidal Oatmeal Shampoo for Dogs

**⅛ cup (30ml) prepared Castile people shampoo, page 81**
**½ cup (228g) colloidal oatmeal**
**Small amount of bitter apple**

If you make your own colloidal oatmeal, boil ½ cup (117g) ground oatmeal with ½ cup (120ml) water. You can apply directly to the pet or add the oatmeal to the shampoo and use as a mix. Add the bitter apple. Make and use immediately.

## Flea and Tick Shampoo

**Prepared Castile people shampoo, page 81**
**Essential oil of your choice (herbal chart on page 171)**

For a smaller pet —to one tablespoon (15ml) shampoo, add one to two drops essential oil (or total combination of essential oils).
For a larger pet — to two to three tablespoons (30ml to 45ml) shampoo, add three to four drops total essential oils.

Store in a bottle labeled with name and make date.

Shelf Life: 6 months

# Dry Oatmeal Shampoo

(dogs or cats)

½ cup (110g) baking soda
¼ cup (32g) corn starch or rice flour
½ cup (110g) colloidal or finely ground oatmeal (regular oatmeal ground in food processor)
3 to 4 drops essential oil

Use an old-fashioned hand sifter to sift the dry ingredients together. Force the essential oil into the dry ingredients through the sifting process. Place in a covered container labeled with name and make date. Store in a cool dry place.

Shelf Life: 4 to 5 months

Milk and yogurt are nontoxic liquids that help calm hot spots.

Sweet oil also can be used to help calm your animal's irritated skin. The sweet oil helps soothe irritations and gives your pet a shiny coat. When applying the oil, take the opportunity to give your pet a massage; both you and your pet may find this soothing. Since nervousness may be a contributing factor to the skin condition, the massage is a reassurance to your pet and that will help calm and heal him.

*Cats are not fond of water but they love to be brushed. This dry shampoo works by taking the excess body oil and dander out of the animal's coat. Use this recipe as a touch-up for dogs or as a dry shampoo for cats. Sprinkle a little on the animal, then brush out the dry shampoo, oil and grim from your pet's coat. Works to prevent fleas and ticks too if you add a little cedar wood or citronella oil.*

# Dandruff Rinse

1 aspirin
4 drops tea tree oil
½ cup (120ml) water

Crush the aspirin. Add the aspirin to the oil and water. Mix thoroughly. Make and use immediately.

*Make a dandruff rinse for after shampooing. Aspirin is made from an acid that actually is used in commercial dandruff shampoo. It really works, so make your own for you and/or your pet. Pour the dandruff rinse over and into your pet's skin beneath the hair. Let sit for one to two minutes, then rinse with clear water.*

# FLEAS

Make your pet taste bad to fleas and increase their B vitamins at the same time. Brewer's yeast added to your pet's diet makes the animal taste less appealing to the fleas.

Add one or two teaspoons (4g to 8g) of powdered brewer's yeast to your pet's food. Brewer's yeast is also used in the pet treat recipe on page 147. Your pet will love you for it.

## Flea Remover

Mix six drops essential oil to ¼ cup (120ml) olive or sweet almond oil and apply to your pet's skin. Fleas don't like citronella, thyme or cedar wood oil either.

## Flea Science Experiment

Fleas are attracted to light...true or false? You may not want to do this much work, but I heard about this experiment in another book a long time ago and I had an opportunity to try it out when I adopted a dog from the pound. The dog was loaded with fleas and I got quite a few fleas to try the recipe. It's weird, but it does work.

Since most of the remedies are to repel fleas and not kill them (then we would need a pesticide) here is something I tried for fun, just because I could.

Isolate the animal away from other pets so the fleas don't spread. Place the pet on a cedar pet-bed (see tip, left). Put a natural flea collar (homemade or purchased) on the pet. Place a bright light and a large shallow pan of water near the pet's bed late at night. Fleas, not liking the cedar and thyme from the flea collar, jump off the dog.

Fleas are attracted to the warmth and light, I guess the fleas think it is another animal, so they jump toward the light and land in the pan of water and drown. It was a fun experiment; I didn't get all the fleas that way, but I got quite a few. I'm not sure I would take the time to do this again, but it was fun to see that it really did work!

Make your own cedar pet-bed with an old pillowcase. Fill the pillowcase with soft cedar shavings and then sew it together.

I made my own flea collar with a bunch of fresh thyme from the garden. I put the thyme into a cloth and then sewed it together to make a tube. Then, I tied it to the dog.

# MANGE

Mange is a skin condition that's completely different than hot spots. When your pet is scratching and his hair is falling out and he has a bad smell, your pet may have mange. If it is severe or wide-spread, call your vet. If it has just started, sometimes you can deter or even stop the mange by purchasing an over-the-counter lime-sulfur combination available at your pet or feed store. One safe and effective brand is called LymDyp™. You probably will have to repeat the process two or three times to get it all. Remember to also treat your pet to an oatmeal shampoo or sweet-oil treatment to help soothe your poor pet's nerves. Mange causes extreme itching, and by the way, it's also contagious to people so wear gloves. Give them lots of love as they will be confused and miserable until it's gone.

## Antiseptics

My recommendations for natural antiseptic products include tea tree oil or witch hazel for dogs and witch hazel for cats (tree tea oil can be harmful to cats).

# TICKS

These nasty little blood suckers can cause diseases, such as Lyme disease and Rocky Mountain spotted fever. We do not want to mess around with them. To naturally rid your pets of these pests, try garlic. Adding a little garlic to your pet's food will make them unattractive to ticks (and fleas). The old farmers used kerosene to remove ticks, but I prefer tea tree oil or Tabasco® sauce. Never, never, "pull out" the tick. It will break in two leaving the front end still working on your pet which can cause an infection. If you need to remove a tick, this is what I recommend.

## Tick Removal

**Tabasco sauce or tea tree oil**
**Tweezers**
**Cotton swabs**
**Rubber gloves**

Put on the gloves and arm yourself with the tweezers. Calm your pet and get him to lie down, or get someone to help hold him. Generously apply tea tree oil or Tabasco sauce to the back end of the tick. When the tick backs out of the skin, grab it in the middle with the tweezers. Destroy the tick. Usually, you can just pop or squeeze the tick with the tweezers and then dispose of them down the drain or toilet.

# DIGESTIVE UPSETS

## Constipation

Add a little canola oil or vegetable shortening to your pet's food. Depending on the size of the animal, ½ teaspoon (2.5ml) to one tablespoon (15ml) should work. This will provide lubrication and usually get things moving.

## Diarrhea

I'm not sure who this is hardest on — the pet or the owner! My vet says it's fine to give your pet a little Kaopectate® to help stop the flow. Go easy though, Kaopectate contains a clay that helps absorb the excess liquid in the bowel and stabilizes the condition. If you give your pet too much, your pet will get the other problem. I also give my pets Pedialyte®, which is available at discount, grocery and drug stores. Intended for babies, it replaces electrolytes lost through diarrhea and makes pets and people recover and feel better faster. I carry some when I travel to other countries, just in case I have problems. I correct the initial problem, then drink some Pedialyte. It's also available in small powder packets that work great when you're traveling.

# ODORS

Did your pet come in contact with something that smells really nasty like a skunk, or play in a sewer or a ditch? Dogs usually are the guilty party here, but hey, it can happen to anyone. Here are the steps to take to remove the worst smells. It works on pets and people.

*This is some work, but if that smell is skunk...it's worth the effort. If it is a lesser smell, you only may have to do steps 1 and 2, possibly step 3. These ingredients are great for cutting the smell. The acid in the recipe helps start neutralizing the odor.*

## Tough Odor Remover

**Tomato juice**
**Vinegar**
**Crushed onion juice**
**Homemade liquid Castile shampoo, page 81**
**Vanilla oil or extract**
**Optional: Dry Pet Shampoo, page 153**

Place your pet (or person) in a big tub and wash them down with a mix of 50 percent tomato juice and 50 percent vinegar. If you can add some crushed onion juice, it is even better. Let that sit for just a couple of minutes.

Shampoo the tomato-vinegar off. Rinse well. For people, skip the dry pet shampoo.

For pets, use the dry pet shampoo to finish pulling out odor if needed (page 153).

Mix 12 drops of vanilla oil or (one tablespoon (15ml) vanilla extract) in one cup (120ml) water.

Spray on the pet's coat or person's skin. Vanilla helps neutralize any remaining spray and it's nontoxic.

## Cat Litter and Deodorizer

*Make your own cat litter with this recipe. You can double or triple the recipe to make a large amount at one time. This has a long shelf life, although you periodically may have to add more fragrance to refresh. Use as you would ordinary litter.*

Get longer use out of your commercial cat litter by adding baking soda and vermiculite to refresh the litter after it is cleaned.

5 pounds (3kg) sand

2 cups (442g) baking soda

3 cups (84g) vermiculite

6 drops vanilla or pineapple fragrance or essential oil

**COST COMPARISON**
**Homemade: $5.65 for 20 pounds.**
**Arm & Hammer® Super Scoop®: $12.99 for 20 pounds**

## Bad Breath

Dogs are notorious for bad breath. Put a few drops of liquid chlorophyll in their drinking water and it will help clean your pets from the inside out, freshen their breath, and supplement their diet. Parsley is a natural breath cleaner as well. Sometimes, I put both ingredients in my homemade dog treats or offer them parsley, if they will eat it.

## Pet Odor Remover

Animal urine is one of the most challenging smells to get out of flooring. Carpet is the most vulnerable material because the urine travels down through the carpet to the padding and flooring below. There are two basic ways to approach this problem if the smell is strong — on the surface of the carpet and down into the pad and the sub-floor under the carpet. See page 127 for recipe.

## "Oops," Pet Stain Remover

Make your own enzyme-type pet stain remover. Catch that potty spot right away, and chances are you can fix the problem more easily. See page 126 for recipe.

# DENTAL HEALTH FOR PETS

A lot of health problems start in the mouth with tooth problems, both in people and pets. With more and more "pet kids" being treated like people, dental problems, especially in dogs and cats, are on the rise. I know this may sound like a bit much, but many animals do not get enough roughage in their food to help clean the tartar off their teeth as nature intended. Occasionally, brush your pet's teeth to help eliminate tartar. Animals can develop tarter and plaque problems too. Buy a toothbrush of the appropriate size for your pet and make this special pet toothpaste.

*You have to make this toothpaste up every time you need it, but with only two ingredients it's easy.*

## Pet Toothpaste

**1 teaspoon (5g) baking soda**
**2 teaspoons (10ml) milk of magnesia**

Mix together to make a paste. Brush your pet's teeth.

# PET BEHAVIOR

Some pets like the taste of plants and can destroy your pot or container plant by either chewing on it, or, as male dogs sometimes do, use them as a potty. Try the Tabasco or bitter-apple recipes below as a great No-No training device. It teaches the animal to stay away and it doesn't cause any permanent damage. The Tabasco causes the animal no discomfort, and if you can catch them experiencing the displeasure, firmly tell them NO at the same time. It will etch the experience in their memories, and they will remember it is not a pleasant thing to do. Dogs sniffing for a place to go potty will find the smell unappealing and move on.

## Tabasco No-Lick Spray

*Mix and use this spray on plants to protect them from dogs, cats and rabbits. It also can be used on your body, but do not rub your eyes or scratch your nose when it's on your hands — it stings.*

¼ cup (60ml) Tabasco sauce (one small bottle)
1 cup (240ml) water

Mix together and place in a spray bottle. Label with name and make date.

Shelf Life: 4 to 5 months

## Bitter-Apple No-Lick Spray

*You can buy concentrated bitter apple from pet stores, hardware stores with pet sections or feed stores. It is a clear liquid and will not stain anything that normally wouldn't stain with plain water. You also can use it on your shoes, fabric or furniture to discourage chewing.*

I had a dog that loved to lick my bare legs in the summer, and even though I loved the dog, the leg licking became very annoying. I got tired of fighting with the whole "training" thing, so one day, I sprayed my bare legs with bitter apple. When he came up to me to show his oral adoration, I let him lick me once and then yelled, NO! He tried it one more time, looked confused, and never did it again. Now, we enjoy many walks together, side by side, with no leg licks.

For this no-lick spray, mix 50 percent bitter apple with 50 percent water. Pour into a spray bottle. Label with name and make date.

Shelf Life: 3 to 4 months

# CHAPTER FIVE

# INDOOR PLANTS AND PATIO GARDENS

There are many good books on outdoor gardening, but your health, where you live, and the time of year may force you inside more than you would like. Or maybe you're just a garden fanatic and your greenhouse and yard are full and you're still not satisfied. Well take heart; there is a way you can bring a little outdoors inside with indoor gardening. We'll start with making your own potting soil, and then look at lovely and useful plants you can grow indoors to enjoy, and yes, save some money at the same time.

Latin is considered the root language for many of the world's languages and a common source for communication. So it was only natural that Carl Von Linne, a Swedish doctor from the 1700s, used Latin to develop a uniform naming system for plants. With so many varieties of plants and herbs, and new ones being developed all the time, this system creates a common ground for the identification or root word for plant names, preventing any disputes. As a matter of fact, in the year 2000, the FDA mandated that all botanicals listed in personal care products be identified by their Latin names (check your cosmetic and toiletry labels). This allows us, as consumers, to research these products so we can be better informed about what is in the products we are purchasing.

We'll concentrate on two basic types of houseplants, the ornamental and edible types that are most suited to growing indoors. Edible plants that we can grow inside are beautiful to look at but also serve a function. We grow them to eat, enjoy and use in homemade recipes.

When you plant an indoor garden, you'll get personal satisfaction knowing you created a garden that nourishes your eyes, soul and your stomach. Enjoy your creation in wonder and good health. You'll have peace of mind knowing that you control what goes into your food source.

# GROWING INDOOR PLANTS

Some of the ways to save money is to start your own little seedlings and grow your own flowers, plants, herbs and vegetables. (Save your money for larger more expensive plants.) Getting a jump start on the growing season will have you enjoying the fruits of your labor a lot earlier. Nothing tastes better than that first fruit, vegetable or herb picked right out of your indoor or patio container.

# SOIL MIXES, FERTILIZERS AND MORE (the nitty gritty)

I hope you are excited, inspired, and ready for all the peace and pleasure that an indoor garden will bring. But now we need to get into the nitty-gritty — the basics of a successful garden and the cures for what ails it.

An indoors or patio container garden needs light, air, soil and water to grow. Just as with anything worth having in life, you can expect to plan a little, work a little and then enjoy. But what about problems that may arise? Let's discuss a few of them and some possible solutions.

We'll start with soil basics. You can buy potting soil, but then, this book is about self-sustainability and budget-saving ideas. So, let's roll up our sleeves and get to it.

The two soil mixes on page 164 will help your garden grow. They are both good; it just depends on whether the plant calls for a more arid soil. In a perfect situation, which we actually don't get too often, a perfect potting soil would include nitrogen, phosphorus, potash, trace minerals, fertilizer, macrobiotic life, humus, calcium and natural earth. It's OK, really, stay with me and I will make it easier — I promise. I just want to give you some basic soil education.

The following items are needed to enrich the soil.

## Nitrogen

Nitrogen is an essential element for plant vigor and growth. An ongoing supply of good compost and other organic matter should take care of the nitrogen needs for most potting soils. If your plants are slow to grow or have light-green to yellow foliage when they should have dark green leaves, bump up the nitrogen in your soil. You can do this by using blood meal, bone meal or cottonseed meal. Liquid nitrogen is also available at most garden stores. Follow the directions for use.

## Phosphorus

Phosphorus helps promote cell division and root development and is critical to fruit and flower growth. If your plant does fine, but never gets fruit or flowers, you may want to increase the phosphorus or finely-ground phosphate rock in your soil. Phosphorus can be found in bone meal, which also boosts nitrogen.

## Potash (Potassium)

Potash is vital for cell division, helps form strong stems, and helps your plants fight off disease. Do you have lots of spindly plants with yellow-streaked leaves? Add potash and trace minerals, of which I recommend: kelp meal, wood ashes, crushed granite or coffee grounds.

## Trace Minerals

Soil benefits from these micronutrients: boron, chlorine, copper, calcium, iron, magnesium, manganese, molybdenum, sulfur and zinc. These usually are available, but if you want to add more trace minerals, add some liquid kelp.

# Casey's Super-Duper Indoor Potting Soil

*I like to make a lot of this potting soil at one time and put it into a small plastic trash can with a lid. I store it in my garage, and now, it's ready whenever I need to transplant a houseplant.*

Buy inexpensive potting soil and boost it with coffee grounds and bone meal.

**6 cups (1.4kg) topsoil**

**1 cup (227g) sand**

**1 cup (28g) vermiculite**

**2 cups (454g) peat moss**

**½ cup (114g) coffee grounds**

**1 teaspoon (5g) potash**

**1 tablespoon (15g) bone meal**

**¼ teaspoon (1.5g) Epsom salt**

**1 cup compost (if you have access to some)**

Mix and use. If it is an arid plant, change the proportions of the first two ingredients as follows:

Three cups (681g) topsoil, to three cups (681g) sand.

# STARTING FROM SEED

To start seeds from scratch, you'll need little peat starter pots or trays from your local garden store. Small recycled milk cartons or starter pots from a former plant purchase will also work. I'm sure you have plenty of recyclables around your home that are suitable for starting plants.

Make up the special homemade plant mix below, or if your time-strapped, purchase potting soil from your local source. Follow the planting directions on the seed packet. Most varieties of plants have different instructions, have you seen those pre-made seed strips sold in garden stores?

## Indoor Seed-Starter Plant Mix

**Mix equal amounts of both:**

**Peat moss**

**Perlite or vermiculite**

Make a soil blend with the peat moss and vermiculite (both are available at your local garden store or in the garden section of most other stores). Plant your seeds as directed and water well. Keep soil moist until small starts sprout. When they are approximately three inches (8cm), carefully transplant them in their new "pot or container" home.

### LET'S MAKE IT EASY

You get both phosphorus and nitrogen from bone meal, potash from coffee grounds, and trace minerals from liquid kelp.

## Plant Vitamins

*Here's a nutritious additive to add every few months to your plants...a vitamin, if you will.*

*Before adding this vitamin mix to your plants, add one teaspoon (5ml) liquid kelp. Then, toss the mix onto the surface dirt of your plant, as needed (not too often). There, that wasn't so bad now....*

½ cup (114g) **bone meal**
¼ cup (57g) **coffee grounds**

Mix the bone meal and coffee grounds together. Store in a labeled container. Remember to add the liquid kelp when you're ready to add the vitamin mix to your plants.

Shelf Life: 12 months

# EASY INDOORS KITCHEN PRODUCE

This is an easy way to make a plant start from items in your kitchen. It's a great project to do with your kids or just enjoy the process yourself. I am enchanted with the idea that after a special meal with family or friends, I can use something from the occasion to "sprout" a plant that will represent our ongoing relationship — a friendship plant from our meal and time together.

## Avocado

Take the pit from the avocado. Insert three or four toothpicks around the middle. Use the toothpicks to suspend the avocado pit, flat side down, over a glass. Add water until the base of the pit is submerged. Eventually, the pit will crack and the new roots will start to emerge, followed by a stem shooting upward. Cut the stem halfway down when it's about seven inches (18cm) tall to encourage branching. When the stem is about twelve inches (31cm) tall and there is some foliage and plenty of roots, move to a pot filled with moist potting soil. Place in a sunny window. Now you have a "free" avocado plant made from waste (no cost) that you can keep or give to your friend as a gift.

## Sweet Potato

Use inserted toothpicks to suspend the sweet potato over a glass, placing the pointed end of the potato in the water. Keep the potato in a warm, sunny window and soon vines with leaves will appear and climb up your window. Train the tendrils to go where you want them to go using string or wire. Do not transplant to soil. It will get out of control for an indoor plant. Rather, keep the water level constant and trim overgrowth as needed.

### QUICK STINKY FERTILIZER

If you buy canned tuna in water, add a little of the juice to your plants instead of pouring it down the drain. It works as a light, fishy fertilizer. Your plants will love it as long as the cats don't attack your plant. When I fertilize my plants, I put them in a closed room for a day or two until the plant absorbs the fishy smell and it's safe from my cats.

## Sprout an Orange or Grapefruit Tree

Plant seeds from your citrus fruit as soon as you're done eating the fruit. Do not let the seeds dry out. Place them one-half inch (13 mm) down into the potting soil. Water them well and loosely cover with plastic wrap. Place in bright light. Keep moist and warm until the green shoots appear. Remove plastic when the shoots come through. Keep in a bright light and it will grow and grow if you have room and the right location. Otherwise, plant it outside, weather permitting, or give it away to someone who has space for the tree. What fun!

## Ginger

Insert toothpicks into a two- to three-inch (6cm to 8cm) piece of ginger root. Suspend the ginger root horizontally across the top of a glass. Add water until the bottom third the of root is submerged. Roots will sprout first. When the roots are one to two inches (3cm to 6cm), plant in soil just below the surface. Place in a window that gets partial sunlight. Stems and leaves will soon grow.

### WEED DETERRENT

Containers and window gardens are small spaces to weed, but occasionally you get a weed that has small tentacles to the roots and you can't seem to get it all, or you've placed your indoor plants outside for the summer months and when you bring them back into the house it has little outdoor weeds growing in it. Most of the time you can just pull them out. Use an eyedropper to put a few drops of gin on the area of the weed root, keeping it away from your plant's root stalk. The alcohol seals off the root stock to the tiny weed.

# Clean and Shine Houseplant Polish

*This is a great "clean-and-shine" product for removing dust that accumulates on your plants and reviving the plants luster. It's a natural cosmetic for your plants that will give them a healthy glow. Cosmetics for your plants? Sure. Now, just talk to them too and they'll grow like crazy.*

*Keep in mind, a little goes a long way on the leaves. For delicate leaves, spray on a fine mist of polish and then follow with a fine mist of plain water. For large waxy leaves, spray on the mix and then wipe off. This mix has no shelf life, so mix it and use it immediately. Don't be tempted to substitute a mineral oil for the natural oil. The mineral oil will coat the leaves and diminish the plant's carbon dioxide and oxygen exchange. The natural oil allows the plant to breathe. Olive oil and water do not mix well, so you can substitute natural water-soluble bath oil for the olive oil.*

**1 tablespoon (15ml) olive oil**
**1 tablespoon (15ml) baby shampoo (or liquid Castile soap, page 50)**
**3 cups (720ml) warm water**

Pour into a spray bottle and use immediately. Label with name and make date. Continue to shake the bottle each time you use it.

I don't know about you, but it seems that I routinely end up with one mate-less sock after the laundry is all done. Where does it go? A great use for that one leftover sock is to use it for regular dusting of furniture or cleaning windows or mirrors. It's also perfect for wiping off the polish from large leaves.

# Garden Chemical Neutralizer

*A friend of mine, who is sensitive to chemicals, recently received houseplants for a "housewarming" gift and she could smell the strong chemical spray on one of the plants. I made up this neutralizer recipe for her so she could get rid of the pesticide residual. The recipe also neutralizes or detoxifies lawns that may have been chemically treated. The Castile (or baby shampoo) breaks down the chemicals and provides glide to flush the chemicals away more quickly. The sugar contained in the corn syrup also helps break down the chemicals. Rinse well after spraying on the plants or lawn.*

**⅛ cup (29g) corn syrup (light or dark)**
**½ cup (120ml) liquid Castile soap, page 50 or baby shampoo**
**1 gallon (4L) water**

Mix together and store in a container labeled with name and make date.

Shelf Life: 3 to 4 months

# CONTAINERS AND POTS

You don't have to spend a fortune on pots or containers. For your indoor gardening or for plants on your patio, saving money and recycling is best, so get creative. I've listed some alternative containers as suggestions to get you started. Check your garage, a garage sale, or use empty containers from the groceries you've purchased. Reusing is the same as recycling.

You will need to make holes in the bottom of the container to allow for drainage — you don't want to drown your plants with water. Depending on the material of your container, you either can drill holes with a drill or use a hammer and nail to make holes in the bottom. To the bottom of the pot, add about one-half inch (13 mm) of gravel or small stones for an additional drainage barrier. Fill your pot with soil, and transplant your seedlings into their new home.

· Many of these ideas for containers and pots can be recycled from items you no longer use, or were discarded by someone else.

· Teapot or large mug

· Old kettle

· Large plastic soda bottles (cut in half and use the bottom half)

· Milk jugs

· Tires from cars, tractors, wheelbarrows, bikes, etc.

· Fifty-five-gallon drum, cut in half (great for cucumbers on the patio)

· Wooden carpenter's box or gun box

· Hollow piece of driftwood or log

· Picnic basket

· Wooden box

· Boots, rubber, plastic, etc.

· Wheelbarrow

· Old red wagon

· Unused fountain

· Wooden chair with a pot installed in the center

· Wicker baskets

# THYME FOR HERBS

Growing herbs in your indoor garden is easy and there are several herbs you can grow inside all year long. It's a delight for the cook in the family who can pick just what she needs for dinner. Herbs are used fresh or dry and you save a lot of money growing your own. This section on herbs will be useful to you when choosing which herbs, oils or scents you want to use in the many recipes and gift ideas I've provided in this book. Herbs also help with medicinal purposes (many of the recipes in this book use them) as well as in cooking. You can make wonderful herb vinegars, butters and more to enjoy or give as gifts.

The following herbs can be started from seed or you can buy them in small starts and transplant into your own pots. You will notice that some of these herbs grow fairly tall if you do not cut them back, but do not let that scare you from growing them indoors. To truly enjoy your indoor herbs, clip and use your herbs as they grow, keeping them at a very modest six-inch (16cm) height. Considering what dried herbs cost at the store, it would be a shame not to cook with them regularly.

## Rosemary (Ros marinus)

Rosemary is a hardy, tall plant with many uses and beautiful green-gray, skinny, aromatic foliage. It can grow three to three-and-one-half feet (92cm to 107cm) tall and it does well in containers. Rosemary will thrive in less than perfect soils, so completely dry out between waterings. Wonderful in so many things: chicken, lamb, salads, herbed butters and more.

*Rosemary*

## Oregano (Origanuum vulgare)

Make sure the variety you buy is really oregano and not marjoram. Sometimes, because oregano is a little hard to get, companies will substitute marjoram for oregano. (Check the label for the Latin name.) Oregano has a stronger flavor than marjoram and has heart-shaped leaves. Usually, the flowers are soft pink. It grows to a height of about six to twelve inches (16cm to 31cm). It commonly is used in Italian cooking such as pasta dishes and marinara sauce. The oil of pure oregano has been shown to be effective in cosmetic products as well as many healing formulas.

*Oregano*

*Mint*

*Sage*

*Dill*

## Thyme (Thymus vulgaris)

This short, bush-like herb bears pink or white flowers on thin silvery foliage. Clip this herb often and use it to season chicken. (I love a rosemary and thyme combination with chicken.) There are many varieties of thyme such as lemon, caraway and lavender. This aromatic herb grows four to twelve inches (11cm to 31cm) high, depending on the variety. Mix it with oregano in Italian dishes or substitute where you want a milder flavor.

## Marjoram (Majorana hortensis)

This herb is related to oregano. It is milder than oregano and this compact bush can grow one to two feet (31cm to 61cm) high. Marjoram has a delicate flavor and often is used to flavor fish, tomato and pasta dishes. Marjoram's white or pale-pink blooms are attractive and it does well in rich soil and full sun.

## Mint (Mentha)

There are many members in the mint family and I love all of them. Mints are great container plants because their creeping roots can take over a whole garden. Mint goes well with lamb, makes delicious tea, and it's an aromatic, invigorating addition to your bath and skin care recipes. Peppermint also soothes an upset stomach. I like to plant traditional peppermint and spearmint along with several more exotic mints such as chocolate mint, pineapple mint, ginger mints, and others. Most mints will grow up to about two feet (61cm) tall.

## Sage (Salvia officinalis)

There are a few varieties of sage, all beautiful, and they sport a variety of leaf and flower colors. I like to combine the flavors of lemon and sage when cooking. Sage generally is very hardy but requires full sun and well-drained soil. It grows to approximately two feet (61cm) in height. Sage is great with poultry, pork, egg dishes, cooked vegetables and fish.

## Dill (Anethum graveolens)

This attractive annual grows fine, wispy foliage and interesting yellow flowers with a strong scent. All parts of dill are edible and rich in vitamins. Combine fresh dill with onions in watered-down vinegar for a flavorful snack. Dill grows a little over two feet (61cm) tall if not trimmed and likes to dry out between waterings. Used in making pickles, dill is also good with fish and in salads, and it can be combined with cream cheese or sour cream as a dip or vegetable topping.

# Tarragon (Artemisia dracunculus)

Tarragon requires a sunny location and likes to dry out between waterings. It grows to almost two feet (61cm) tall and it has long, narrow leaves. It seems to be odor-free until it's been cut. Wonderful in fish, chicken, stuffing, salads and more.

# Basil (Ocimun basilicum)

Once you try basil, chances are you will fall in love with it. There is sweet basil (my favorite) lemon basil, purple basil, miniature basil and a few others. Basil often is used in soups to boost the wholesome flavor and in other Italian dishes, vegetables and pesto sauces. Minestrone and lasagna are two favorites. This beautiful plant can grow to two feet (61cm) high if not regularly harvested. Basil requires a warm and well-lit location. Most basil is fairly hardy and easy to dry.

# Chives (Allium schoenoprasum)

Chives are a favorite for seasoning food. This little cousin to the onion can be used wherever you would use onion and substituted for onion where onion may be too strong. Chives go great with cottage cheese and it's best when the chives are fresh. Dips, meats, salads, vegetables, and almost every soup benefit from chives. This wispy grass-looking plant with white flowers can grow up to one-and-one-half feet (46cm), so clip and use it often. Chives love full sun or part sun, and like the onion, they like moist soil. Remove flower stalks after they bloom. This herb can be used fresh, dried or frozen.

# Parsley (Petroselinum crispum)

Iron-rich with lots of vitamins, parsley is great for eating and it's used as a natural breath purifier. There are many kinds of this easy-to-grow herb. Parsley is used as a garnish in restaurants for a colorful topping to salads or sprinkled on for a decorative look. Don't be stingy with this herb — if you see it on your plate — eat it. Parsley has so many health benefits, yet most people think of it as just a garnish. It is a little challenging to grow from seed because it has an unusually long germination time, but little plant starts are inexpensive. This herb likes sun and medium-damp soil. It will grow up to one foot (30cm) if you don't trim it, so make sure you do. Use it and enjoy!

# Chamomile (Anthemis nobilus)

Chamomile often is used in teas. (It makes a relaxing tea if you are stressed.) My mother used to grow it and make tea from the delicate little blooms. She would brew it for me and add a little milk and honey to help promote a restful night of sleep or for a little stress relief during the day. Chamomile can grow between one to two feet (30cm to 61cm). It has dainty, thin foliage with small, daisy-like flowers from which you make the herbal tea. It is a delicate-looking and fragrant herb that sometimes is used as a ground cover.

*Tarragon*

*Basil*

*Chives*

## Bay Leaf (Laurus nobilus)

This herb is actually a shrub and it was cherished by the ancient Romans for both culinary and decorative purposes. Start it small and keep it trimmed and manageable in a pot. If you don't, it can grow into a small tree. Bay leaf is a very slow grower. Rich, green leaves give excellent flavor to stews and soups. It is hardy in most soils and likes to dry out between waterings. The leaves are easy to harvest and dry.

## Chervil (Anthriscus cerefolium)

The Romans introduced chervil to England where it became quite popular. It was one of the Roman's favorite herbs. It is a low-growing plant that prefers semi-shade and grows about one foot (30cm) tall. This herb has very delicate foliage and dainty white flowers, and sometimes, like chamomile, it is used as a ground cover. Chervil is an important ingredient in béarnaise sauce and it's good in salads and soups or with chicken or fish. This delicate herb easily loses its flavor, so do not cook it, or if you do, don't expose it to heat for a long time.

## Catnip (Nepeta cataria)

Not just for cats, this pretty herb makes a good tea for you to enjoy. If you are a cat lover, your cat will love you if you grow it fresh for them. It is richly aromatic, and you will need to keep kitty away from the growing plant until it is ready to harvest, or kitty will just pounce on the plant and make short work of it. It's best if you grow and harvest, then start over with a new plant. Cats will enjoy the leaves dry or fresh. Tall with pink or white flowers (it's the leaves kitties like the most).

# EDIBLE FLOWERS

Why not create a "potpourri" for your tummy. Indoor gardening also can include edible flowers. If you've never tried eating flowers, give it a try. It seems odd at first, but most are quite good. Try them fresh in a colorful garden salad. Other fun ideas include freezing the flower petals in ice cubes to float in punch bowls, individual drinks of iced tea, lemonade or other summer drinks... charming!

In Victorian times edible flowers were all the rage. The flower's petals were lightly coated with egg whites, dusted with sugar and then left to dry. They were eaten like a candy or used as an edible summer cake decoration. This method is still done today.

Following are some edible flowers that can be grown indoors and enjoyed.

## Nasturtium (Tropaeolum)

This flower has beautiful green or marbled green-and-cream leaves that are delicious and beautiful in salads. The flowers, in colors of red, yellow and peach, are also edible with a light texture and taste. Smaller varieties grow to about one foot (30cm) tall, but climbing varieties grow to greater heights. Nasturtiums can be cross-planted with tomatoes. The climbing nasturtium will wind around the tomatoes, but not overpower the plant. It will look like an unusual tomato plant with both flowers and fruit coming from it. Plant in a pot on your deck for good food and decoration. For indoor gardening, stay away from the climbing variety and purchase little bush plant varieties.

## Roses (Rosaceae)

Standard-size roses are too big for indoors, but there are lovely miniature roses that do very well indoors. Despite the tiny thorns, rose flowers are beautiful and sweet to eat (only the flowers are edible). In Victorian times, candied (sugared) roses often were used on foods; rose water and glycerin softened our great-grandmothers' skin, and rose teas were popular. Roses come in a wide variety of colors. Do not wait too long to pluck the blooms. They taste best when first in full bloom or as maturing buds.

## Borage (Borago officinalis)

The borage leaves, when cooked, will remind you of spinach. Borage is hardy and prefers full sun. It needs to be trimmed often to keep it to a pot size. Pinch back the leaves on a regular basis to keep the plant under control. The blue flowers from this plant also are edible.

## Pot Marigolds (Calendula)

Colors of off-white, orange and yellow add color to salads and other foods. Marigolds grow up to two feet (61cm) tall and are fairly hardy.

Note: French marigolds are NOT edible, so check with a Master Gardener to make sure you have the edible variety.

# CONTAINER VEGETABLES

Certain vegetables are easy to grow in pots with enough light, water and a little care. You can grow container vegetables almost anywhere in and around the house, or in combination with herbs and edible flowers. What a beautiful and functional display of your "green thumb!" When you are growing plants indoors, you may need a grow light and your home temperature should be adequate. If you are growing vegetables on your deck, patio or porch, plant them in the appropriate season.

## Food, Veggies and Fruit Cleaner

*This recipe will remove pesticide residue. Wash your veggies with the cleaner, then rinse well. The cleaner doesn't have a long shelf life, but it's very easy to make.*

**1 teaspoon (7g) light corn syrup**
**¼ teaspoon (1.5ml) liquid Castile soap (unscented only)**
**16 ounces (480ml) water**

Store in a bottle labeled with name and make date.

Shelf Life: 1 to 2 weeks

## Tomatoes (Lycopersicon esculentum)

There are many kinds of new tomato hybrids in a variety of sizes, shapes and colors as well as heirloom varieties. Start from seed, or buy a new little start in the spring when they are available at your local nursery or the garden section of the store. They need a lot of light and water, but once they start producing, it is likely you will harvest plenty. There is nothing quite like a fresh homegrown tomato.

The most popular tomatoes for container gardens are the cherry-tomato varieties. You will need to make a support for your tomato plant to keep the plant straight as it grows with all the added weight from the lovely tomatoes.

## Peppers (Capsicum frutescens or Capsicum annuum)

Like tomatoes, there are many hybrids of peppers, and most of these plants are low-growing, beautiful, and producers of lots of peppers. Look for small pepper varieties for your indoor or patio container garden.

## Green Onions (Allium cepa)

Just as with chives, you need to cut off the tops of the plants to keep them growing for a long time They like a lot of water.

## Cucumbers (Cucumis sativus)

The cucumber plant grows very large and lengthy, but I have grown a single plant in a large container on the deck. Cucumbers are not recommended for indoors. There are varieties of bush cucumbers that work well in containers and the plants provide many cukes or pickles for a long time.

# COOL-WEATHER CROPS

I grow cool-weather crops such as kale, lettuce, spinach and chard in the garage with a grow light. It's cooler there than in the house. This works best if your garage does not dip below 40°F (5°C) and it warms up to 50°F (10°C) to 70°F (21°C) during the day.

## Kale (Brassica oleracea acephala)

In shades of red, green, white, pink and purple, this plant is one of the most dramatic and beautiful vegetables. Kale is low-growing and looks like an ornamental plant, but you can harvest the leaves for salads or cooked vegetable dishes. Kale is regarded as a winter vegetable and grows in part sun and cooler temperatures.

## Lettuce (Lactuca sativa)

I keep lettuce growing indoors year-round with two to three different plantings. Clip the leaves down about halfway a couple of times a week and the leaves will grow back.

## Spinach/Chard (Spinacia oleracea, Beta vulgaria cicla)

Treat spinach and chard just like lettuce. Cut off the tops and only eat the tops. Keep the crop going for some time by forcing additional plant growth. There are many varieties available.

# ORNAMENTAL CONTAINER PLANTS

Ornamentals are beautiful and functional. They help clean our indoor air to make it healthier, and they decorate and create a peaceful environment in our home.

Along with herbs that beautify and season our food, ornamental plants provide a relaxing atmosphere, add beauty to a room and they are portable. You can have a little garden anywhere, whether you live in an apartment, condo, or a home with a small yard. If you rent, the portable plants can move with you, so once you've invested, you don't have to leave your landscape behind.

Small, single containers can enhance a windowsill, porch or deck. Depending upon where you live, create a bowl with succulents or a wide assortment of wet-weather grasses that move in the wind. Also, cluster several containers into groupings or plant more than one variety into a single container. Use these potted plants to create an inviting private entrance, hide a bare wall, or to landscape the back deck. These ideas for spaces outside of your home will provide beautiful scenery where none existed.

But what about "greening" your inside space? You can do this cost-effectively by hanging plants that need humidity in your kitchen or bathroom, or locate plants requiring a drier existence to other living spaces. They will not ask for much, just give them light, water and fertilize one to two times a year and they will love you back with abundant foliage and beautiful flowers. If the plants get too big, prune them back or give them a bigger pot. They will give you pleasure and be good company; you can talk to them and they will love

it. They will listen to your most intimate secrets and tell no one.

Choose an ornamental plant layout that suits your style. Scatter one or two around your house or dedicate a special space for them in your home. A friend of mine, who has an extra bedroom, winters-over her herbal and ornamental stock in an open-faced closet and enjoys her indoor garden all winter long. She took off the closet doors, hung grow lights in the top of the closet and put in tiered shelves so all the plants could get some light.

Suspend your plants and foliage overhead if you don't have any floor space to accommodate them. If you don't want to put holes in the walls, hang the plant hook on a reinforced curtain rod, or buy an old-fashioned bird-cage hanger and hang a plant from it.

Wherever you plan to display your plants, think about how you can combine different types of plants to create a mix of textures, shapes and colors for an interesting effect. Another secret for making your "garden-like" display is to vary vertical (tall) and horizontal (short and wide) plants to look more like nature. You also can make or purchase plant towers. These towers have staggered shelves or holders to place plants around a tall stand that doesn't take much room, but holds a variety of plants.

For more inexpensive potted plant ideas, look at the suggestions on page 170.

## Forcing Bulbs Indoors

Some bulbs are more suited to this than others. For this process, you will need pots at least five to six inches (13cm to 16cm) deep. If you are forcing more than one bulb per pot, bulbs need to be placed one to one-and-one-half inches (3cm to 4cm) apart. Once your dried bulbs are potted, keep them slightly moist during the growing process. There are many varieties of bulbs sold with a pot and dirt ready for you to plant, water and watch grow. Some of the easiest plants to force a bloom indoors are amaryllis, callas, caladiums, hyacinths and crocus. Certain tulips also use this same process. There will be planting and growing directions when you purchase the bulbs. If you need help or don't understand the directions, speak to a store representative or garden specialist. By forcing bulbs indoors, you can have beautiful spring colors on your windowsill year-round.

## Window Gardens

What does your mind envision when you hear those words? Well, there are plenty of ways to create a window garden. If you own your own space and have the extra money, you can install a window greenhouse in one of your windows. This is delightful, but look around for the alternatives as well. Do you have a sunny, bay window or a big, picture window and not too much furniture? Dress up the area by hanging a flower basket on each side of the window and place a table below the window and line it with plants. You'll look through a garden-framed window and always have a touch of summer.

Try any of the following blooms for your indoor window garden:

- Geraniums
- Begonias
- Dwarf marigold
- Nasturtium

**Hardy green plants:**

- Spider plant
- Dracaena
- Chinese evergreen
- Howea forsteriana

# Greenery

The following plants will provide a variety of greenery for decorating your home:

- Zebra plant
- Araucaria
- Bromeliads
- Caladium
- Kangaroo vine
- Citrus trees
- Coleus
- Dumb-cane
- Dracaena (Dragon plant)
- Ficus
- Baby's tears
- Hoya (wax plant)

**Varieties of palms:**

- Philodendron
- Pilea
- Umbrella tree
- Purple heart
- Piggyback plant
- Wandering jew

There may be other plants in your area that are suitable to grow indoors as well, but this list will get you started. Occasionally, rotate your houseplants in your window garden to other areas in your home to liven up a room for a week or two, then return them to their light source.

# Low-light Plants

If you live in the rust-belt like me, and you have a winter without much sun, then choose some of these low-light plants and give them supplemental lighting with a grow light, if needed.

- Deifembacjoa
- English ivy
- Rubber plant/Fiddleleaf fig
- Fatshedera
- African violets
- Ferns
- Pandanus

# Low-maintenance Plants

Travel a lot, forget to water and have a good sunny window? Succulents are perfect for you. Cacti and other desert plants like the sun but will go long periods between waterings. There are many varieties, and some bloom from time to time. Ask your garden retailer to show you some of the varieties they have to offer.

# CHAPTER SIX
# PESKY PESTS
# AND REPELLENTS

In the city or in the country, we love nature and all of the creatures of the world — but sometimes — we need to have them gone!

A love of life, people, nature, animals...we could go on and on there are so many things in this world to appreciate. There are a few things though, that maybe we don't love so much. I realize that several of our earth's creeping members are good for the earth, very helpful and often necessary; however, these little creatures can get out of control and tip the balance of nature or come indoors where they don't belong.

Ridding your indoor garden space or home environment of these pests can be a challenge. I am sure you have read or heard about the dangers of many fertilizers and pesticides. Some of the more commonly used inorganic pesticides are neither pet nor people friendly. These include chlorinated hydrocarbons such as DDT, lindane, chlordane, heptachlor and aldin, just to name a few. Although these chemicals usually are used in graded dosages, then blended back to be moderately low in toxicity to animals and humans, these compounds do not leave our environment quickly. Some take more than a decade to degrade and some end up in our water supplies. These chemicals can build up in concentrations over time on our earth and in our food chain and our bodies. I could belabor this indefinitely to truly build a case for safer natural solutions to irritating pest problems. Trust that this small amount of information regarding some commercial pesticides does just that. I have borrowed time-honored solutions from the knowledgeable Western farmers around me. Some of these solutions have been handed down from generation to generation, while others are newer inventive solutions. Still others are adaptations of commercial products that may not be altogether natural, but are less toxic and less expensive than their commercial cousins. The choices, as always, are up to you. All the following are effective and easy to make.

# PEST MANAGEMENT

Mold, mealy bugs and strains of fungus are truly disgusting. I think I dislike mold and mealy bugs the most — they hurt my pretty houseplants and container plants. Here are some simple solutions to make them go away. Use the solution to wash down the plant leaves that are affected. Then, put a little into the top inch of soil around the plant. It will repel mealy bugs and help kill the mold on plant leaves and the topsoil around the plant.

## Mold and Mealy Bug Wash

½ cup (114g) cup Epsom salt
1 cup (240ml) warm water

Put the Epsom salt into the warm water. Stir until dissolved. Make and use immediately.

## Mildew, Mold and Mealy Bug Spray

1 teaspoon (5ml) liquid Castile soap (store-bought or homemade, page 50)
1 teaspoon (5ml) tea tree extract
3 teaspoons (14g) baking soda
2 quarts (2L) water

Pour the Castile soap, tea tree extract and baking soda into the water. Mix well. Store in a spray bottle. Label with name and make date.

Shelf Life: 3 to 4 months

One of the most famous fungicides in the world is known as Bordeaux mixture. It was discovered when French botanist, Alexis Millardet, noticed that certain grapevines in France were not suffering from mildew. He asked the farmer why, and was told that the grapes, which had a blue tinge on the leaves, had been sprayed with a mixture of copper sulfate (bluestone) and lime to cut down on the pests in the area from pilfering the fruit. This was quite a discovery as it turns out that copper is toxic to the fungus. The addition of lime adheres the mix to the vine and helps reduce the chance of getting too much copper on the plant which would be toxic. Look for copper sulfate "bluestone," or commercial sprays that contain it, at your local garden stores. As a shortcut, buy ready-made Bordeaux mixture in garden stores. If you cannot find it, here is a recipe to make your own "Bordeaux mixture." Lightly spray mixture on plants.

## Fungus Stopper

3 tablespoons (43g) copper sulfate (bluestone)
2 tablespoons (29g) lime
1 cup (240ml) warm water

Mix the ingredients together. Pour in a spray bottle. Label with name and make date. Store in a cool dark place.

Shelf Life: 1 to 2 weeks

## GARDEN FLY TRAP

Those pesky flies! They can get into your house, swarm your picnic area and ruin your grill-out on the deck. Attract them to another area to eliminate the count around your home. Whiteflies and common black flies are attracted to bright colors. Paint small wood stakes bright yellow; according to research, the flies are attracted to this color. Then, smear the stake with something sticky such as petroleum jelly, or wrap the pole like a candy cane with a commercial flycatcher strip. I like the flycatcher strip. It's a nontoxic alternative and it's simple to make — brown paper and a sticky adhesive to catch the flies. You also can hang them in garden rooms. Place the stakes among your potted plants around your deck or porch and decrease the population.

## Roach Killer

*Boric acid can be found at the pharmacy. It is toxic to humans and pets — only when it is consumed. Keep it away from animals and small children. Compared with other toxic substances, boric acid is much safer and it does the job. This mixture is a natural toxic feast to these deplorable pests. Place the little balls in places where roaches like to hang out. As a paste, use it to stuff into little concrete cracks or holes where you think the roaches are entering. The sugar and cornstarch attract the roaches to the feast and the shortening holds the compound together and keeps the boric acid in the roach system.*

**2 teaspoons (9g) boric acid**
**2 teaspoons (9g) sugar**
**2 teaspoons (6g) cornstarch**
**2 teaspoons (9g) solid vegetable shortening**

Thoroughly mix all the ingredients. Form into little balls. Place in a container labeled with name and make date. Keep out of the reach of children and pets.

Shelf Life: 3 to 5 months

**$ COST COMPARISON**
**Homemade: $4.84 for 14 ounces**
**Eco-SMART™ Ant & Roach Killer: $13.10 for 14 ounces**

Roach hotels, nontoxic little boxes that the roaches enter but cannot get out of, are available at stores. Throw the box away when finished.

## Simple Homemade Insecticide

*Detergent is toxic to most bugs and the oil makes the detergent stick to them; most will avoid it. Coat leaves of the affected plants, or pour a ring around the plant if they keep invading. You have to repeat this process often as you are mainly repelling the bugs and only killing a few. It may take up to 30 days of repeated applications to get them all — but it is not toxic!*

**2 tablespoons (30ml) liquid dish-washing detergent (strongest, harshest you can find)**
**3 tablespoons (45ml) vegetable oil (liquid cooking oil, any kind)**

Mix and shake well. Pour into a spray bottle. You will have to shake often. Make and use immediately.

## Aphids and Whitefly Repellent

*Spray on plant every two days until the problem is gone.*

**3 tablespoons (45ml) water**
**1 tablespoon (15ml) rubbing alcohol**

Mix and put into a spray bottle labeled with name and make date.

Shelf Life: 1 to 2 months

## Beetle Spray

*What do beetles and vampires have in common? They both detest garlic! This nontoxic (to people and pets) solution will not actually kill the aphids, but it will get them off your plants. They find these ingredients distasteful. I had a dog that liked to chew on my plants but stopped when I applied this repellent. He found the leaves distasteful and left the plants alone — beetles are not the only creatures this repels. To use, simply spray on the beetles (aphids also hate this).*

If you use a food processor to chop onion and garlic, save the juice and put it into this recipe.

**½ onion, finely chopped**
**1 garlic clove, peeled and finely chopped**
**½ cup (120ml) water**

Mix the ingredients in a spray bottle and let it sit overnight. Shake it a few times. You want the garlic and onion to permeate the water with their juices. Label the bottle with name and make date.

Shelf Life: Up to 1 week

## Top-Notch Yellow-Jacket Trap

Yellow jackets can become very aggressive and annoying in the late summer and early fall. Many a picnic has moved indoors because of them. It is hard to kill a yellow jacket without a toxin or physical force (and then you risk getting stung). Some farmers have been using this method for years to get rid of yellow jackets when they become bothersome. The first time my husband made one of these, I laughed when he hung it in a tree, but I was astonished at how well it worked — just as well, if not better, than the expensive traps sold in stores.

The trap works because the yellow jackets are greedy meat eaters. The more fragrant/pungent the meat the better they like it. When they find the meat, fresh or old, the yellow jackets will eat the meat until they become so heavy they fall down into the water and drown. (Maybe there should be a fable about gluttony based on these guys.) In the late summer, the bottom of the trap gets so full of yellow jackets we have to replace it several times. Don't replace the trap, just dump out the dead yellow jackets, refill with water, wire on new meat if needed and re-hang. Hang one of these inexpensive and effective traps where you picnic, and you'll encourage these pests to attend their own "lethal" feast, leaving you to dine in peace.

**Clean plastic gallon (4L) milk jug**
**6" to 8" (16cm to 21cm) pliable wire**
**3 in² to 4 in² (19cm² to 26cm²) piece of raw meat**
**Water**

Cut a triangular hole in the front of the jug on the side opposite the handle, about six inches (16cm) down from the top. Wire the raw meat so that it suspends from the top of the milk jug. To secure, wrap the wire around the neck of the jug or poke holes into the neck and secure the wire into the hole. The meat should dangle inside the top of the jug. Fill the bottom of the jug with water until the water is about an inch (25mm) below the cut-out triangle. Hang the trap off to the side of your picnic and garden areas.

$ **COST COMPARISON**
**Homemade: $1.13 for one gallon (with recycled milk container)**
**RESCUE® Disposable Yellow-Jacket Trap: $9.99 for one gallon trap**

## Bees

There are many species of bees, and for thousands of years humans have enjoyed the benefits of bees. They pollinate our plants and provide us with honey, propolis, bee pollen and beeswax that we use and consume for pleasure and health. It is important to recognize honeybees as friends in the garden, so you don't want to kill them when they come around the picnic table or into your potted container garden.

Honeybees and bumblebees are the only regular collectors of both nectar and pollen. Honeybees are the most important of the pollinating insects, and interestingly enough, work just one kind of flower at a time. They usually are nonaggressive and only sting when threatened — and then they die. You may need to hold them at bay around your eating area or if you are allergic to their sting. Here is a humane way to tell them to buzz off.

Place several commercial, fabric-softener dryer sheets around the area where you plan to be eating. Apparently, the ingredients in the dryer sheets are distasteful to bees.

## Slugs — UGH!

*Two methods work to rid yourself of these slime makers. They can get into your potted garden and make a mess of your pots or leave slimy trails across your deck or patio. The next time you head out after the rain, take along your saltshaker. The challenge is you actually have to see the slug for this to work. Put a generous amount of salt on their tail and they are toast. This works immediately.*

*If they keep leaving their trails and you cannot catch up with the culprit and salt its tail, try this "party night" recipe and they will be gone. This is my favorite because it works as a trap and you do not have to hang around and watch.*

Find a pan with sides no higher than one-and-one-half inches (4cm) or the slug will not be able to crawl in. Pour at least an inch (3cm) depth of beer into the pan. Leave it overnight where you suspect the slugs may travel. Try to find a sheltered area so the beer won't be diluted by rain. Slugs are natural alcoholics and will crawl to the beer, get in the pan, consume enough to become lethargic and then drown. Note: Slugs do not seem to have a brand preference.

# Mosquitoes, Ticks and Flies...Oh My!

*Any camper will tell you these pests are the worst part of any camping trip, although you also can get eaten alive in your backyard or on your patio. This summer, be prepared and make your own repellent for pennies on the dollar. It's safer than many of the commercial brands. You also can spray it on clothes with the exception of silk or other water-sensitive fabrics. Make this nontoxic spray and protect yourself and your family this summer when camping, working in the garden, picnicking on your porch or at the baseball game. You'll enjoy your outing a lot more.*

1 cup (240ml) witch hazel
6 drops pennyroyal essential oil
8 drops citronella essential oil
4 drops eucalyptus essential oil

Pour the witch hazel into a spray bottle. Add the remaining ingredients with an eyedropper. Shake well to mix the ingredients. Label with name and date. Shake before each use.

Shelf Life: Approx. 5 months

Avon's Skin So Soft™ is a commercial product that is less toxic than most bug sprays and you can get it in towelettes. Bugs do not like the fragrance of this product and it works pretty well on mosquitoes. I normally do not like scented items, but this product smells a lot nicer than most bug sprays.

# Along Came a Spider

Most spiders are harmless but beneficial to nature because they prey upon flies, crickets and other insects. Spiders and bats actually are part of Mother Nature's bug-control squad. In the garden, spiders may be unattractive, but they are helpful. If they bother you while you are outside, hose them away. Most spiders are nonaggressive and will try to avoid you, and as a rule, they do not eat your plants.

Consider the following to manage unwanted spiders. Install a sodium vapor light around exterior doors and other entrances. The lights are less attractive than incandescent lights to night-flying insects. And, since most spiders are attracted to places with lots of flies and night-flying insects, you will control your spider population naturally, as they need areas to find their food.

# NATURAL INSECT REPELLENTS

## Alcohol

Rubbing alcohol works the best. The fumes repel pests and kill certain varieties. Store rubbing alcohol in a glass spray bottle and spray them. I have caught flies in mid-air! Vodka also works but not as well (it is not as strong).

## Cedar Wood

Repels fleas and moths.

## Citronella

Mosquitoes and gnats find citronella repulsive and flies are not fond of it either.

## Coffee Grounds

Repels gnats.

## Eucalyptus

Repels gnats and mosquitoes.

## Garlic and Onions

Aphids are very repelled by these and several species of other small bugs don't like them either. If you consume enough garlic, it does emit from your pores. If you eat a lot, the mosquitoes probably will leave you alone...but then, so will everyone else.

## Lemon Juice or Lemon Oil

Cotton or mealy bugs run fast from lemon. Just a dab will do it. Lemon concentrate is very acidic and will "burn" soft-backed bugs.

## Lime Sulfur

Lime sulfur should be handled with care as it's a very effective insecticide. Make a mixture of 50 percent lime sulphur and 50 percent sugar. Store in a labeled bottle with name and make date. It attracts, then kills cockroaches. Lime sulfur can also kill moles and mice. Always follow the warning instructions on the package and keep out of the reach of children and pets. Lime sulphur is available at garden shops.

## Pennyroyal

A repellent for several kinds of winged pests such as flies.

## Pyrethrum Powder

Made of African pyrethrum flowers, this natural powder is effective against chewing and sucking insects. This is also a natural toxin. Read label directions and keep away from children and pets. It is available at garden centers.

## Thyme

Fleas are repelled by thyme.

## Tobacco

It is the nicotine in tobacco that bugs hate (are they smarter than us?). Tobacco has long been known as a natural bug repellent and it is especially effective on lice.

## Tabasco/Hot Mustard

Used concentrated in carrier oils, such as canola and olive oil, this product can be used to coat the leaves of plants to ward off insects, rabbits, domestic pets and deer. Use approximately 30 percent hot mustard or Tabasco to the oil. If you are using this mix on edible items, such as herbs or vegetables, make sure you wash off the mix before eating, or you may be the one repelled. Shake well. Store in a spray bottle and label with name and make date.

Shelf Life: 6 months.

## Sulfur

Repels ticks and helps remove them.

## Vanilla Bean

Repels gnats.

# CONTROLLING BIGGER PESTS

Squirrels, birds, bunnies and other small animals are fun to watch but we do not want them eating our container veggies or herbs. Keeping larger pests out of the pots near the house may sound easy, but in some areas when food foraging gets scarce, or in the case of neighbors (or you) feeding them, they become quite bold.

Keeping them out can be a challenge if you want to do it in a humane way. Years ago, the view out of my bedroom window was my father-in-law's garden. My loving in-laws were our neighbors and it amazed me that I never saw a scarecrow in my father-in-law's garden. His garden area was behind his house out of his sight. One time, I asked him, "Don't you have trouble with birds and bunnies in the garden?" He always had plenty of produce in the summer for his family and ours. I liked his answer, he told me his plan was always to plant more than enough to feed everyone around the garden — humans and varmints alike.

That's probably not possible in our container garden, so here are some ways to keep the "varmints" out.

## Fly Away Birds

The best control method I can recommend is to frighten birds away. The change has been made from the traditional scarecrow to lots of those fun whirligigs sold at garden and gift shops — the movement scares away the birds. Another simple idea is to tie a white plastic garbage bag to a pole and the bag will randomly move with the wind. When movement fails, some people resort to chicken-wire fencing to enclose their garden. If you are a city dweller, you may find that one or two birds in the garden don't eat too much and they're pretty to look at so it doesn't bother you. Or, just do what Grandpa Earl does; plant extra to share with neighbors and critters.

## Attracting Birds

What if you want to attract birds to your patio or porch? You can encourage birds to come to your window with little bird feeders that suction on the window, or with pretty little bird baths and bird feeders set at the end of your deck or patio. A birdhouse also works if you have an undisturbed area. Birds eat insects, so if you have fruit or vegetable containers they can help with pest control. Wrens and robins are especially useful for this and are among the easiest birds to attract.

## Mice and Moles

These small critters can get in your house and scare you, tear up that little patch of lawn, eat your tulip bulbs and nibble at your potted vegetables. You can buy humane traps that will trap small mice and moles and then you have to remove them to a faraway location, but usually they keep coming back. Mix up a batch of this if you want to do away with them.

*Pour this mixture down a mole hole or in mice holes behind cabinets. This mix is only toxic if consumed — and they will consume it. In a short time, the toxins will build up in their systems and kill them.*

## Critter Be Gone

¼ cup (57g) lime sulfur

¼ cup (57g) borax

½ cup (113g) whole-grain flour

¼ cup (35g) corn meal

½ to ¾ cup (103g to 154g) solid vegetable shortening

Using an old spoon, cut the shortening into the dry goods. Wearing rubber gloves, roll the mixture into litle balls. Store this mixture in a well-labeled container and keep out of the reach of children and pets.

Shelf life: 12 months

# Mole and Mice Repellent

*If you want mice and moles to stay away from an area, make and use this repellent. You have to know where their holes are located. Pour into the mole or mouse hole outside. The mix smells nasty to them, ruins their appetite, and usually they just move on. Sounds like a nasty mess, and it is, but it is nontoxic. Reapply after it rains.*

**2 tablespoons (30ml) castor oil**
**6 tablespoons (90ml) liquid dish-washing soap**
**1 teaspoon (5ml) Tabasco**
**1 mashed garlic clove**
**1 quart (960ml) water**

Mix all the ingredients together. Add to the quart of water. Make and use immediately.

## WHEN PETS BECOME GARDEN PESTS

Some pets like the taste of plants and can destroy your container or potted plant by either chewing on them, or as male dogs sometimes do, use them as a potty. Try the Tabasco or bitter-apple trick as a great No-No training device; it works, causes no permanent damage and will teach them to stay away. The Tabasco causes them discomfort, and if you can catch them experiencing the displeasure of it and tell them firmly NO at the same time, it will etch the displeasure in their memories. Dogs sniffing to go potty will find that it is not a smell that appeals to their need to potty in that spot and will move on.

For more pet solutions, see Chapter 4, page 143.

# HOMEMADE GIFT IDEAS

All of the products in this book are natural alternatives to the chemical-laced products on the market. Make a wonderful gift basket for any special occasion. I've offered some suggestions for the occasions and the products that would make the gift special. Get creative!

## Birthday or Spa Gifts

Three to four homemade soaps, facial cleansers, moisturizers etc. Add a nice terry towel or head wrap, soy candles and a few essential oils.

## New Mom/Baby Shower Box

Three to four comfort items for personal care. For new mom or baby shower, add two baby products and one pamper product like stretch-mark oil. Add cloth diapers, there are some great new ones on the market.

## Housewarming

Plant an herb in an old teapot, or make a little window garden planter box. Add seed packets and a bag of potting soil. Three to four cleaning products with a gift certificate and this book.

## Your Man's Birthday or Father's Day

Aftershave, foot powder, one massage oil and a massage gift certificate. Add a personalized note for a soothing back rub.

## Kid's Birthday

Smelly-belly bears in a little basket. One blue bubble bear and one pink crystal bear. Make it boy or girl specific. Add a few bath toys or their own special towel or washcloth.

## Spring Welcome Wagon

Assorted cleaning products and an herb or ornamental plant. Add a few gardening tools or gloves and bug repellents. Create a small patio container with some cherry-tomato plants or bush cucumbers.

## Gardener's Gift Basket

Three to four gardening products, repellents, etc. with one or two small garden tools and gardening gloves. Add some homemade potting soil and a few seed packets or small plants.

## A Starter Herb Garden

Make up mini-pots with planted herbs and garden tools. Add some herb-scented essential oils.

## New Puppy Gift Set

Homemade treats, puppy toy, (knotted extra sock) and two pet-care products. A nice picture frame for their new pet's first photo.

## New Kitty Gift Set

Homemade kitty treats, homemade catnip toy and two care products. Again, a little picture frame for their new kitty and a few other essential ingredients to make their own cat litter. Or, make and package some to add to the gift basket.

## Holidays

This could be a duplicate of any of the above. Design the gift basket to the recipient's likes or needs. Add essential oils with holiday scents, such as cinnamon, wintergreen and peppermint.

# GLOSSARY

**Absorbent/Absorption**: Ability to absorb or transfer of one ingredient/base by another product.

**Accelerator**: Any ingredient or group of ingredients that speeds action or absorption.

**Acid**: Having a pH number below 7.0; the opposite of an alkali. Alkali has a pH number above 7.0.

**Acupressure**: An ancient way of healing by applying pressure to assigned pressure points on the body.

**Alpha Hydroxy Acid (AHA)**: A naturally occurring organic acid such as glycolic acid. Fruit-based anti-aging antioxidant sometimes combined with phospholipids and acidophilus. Skin cell renewal and cell shedding. Glycolic acid is found in simple sugars. Glycolic acid works by dissolving the intercellular cement responsible for abnormal discoloration of the skin and improving skin hydration by enhanced moisture.

**Almond Meal**: Abrasive used as an exfoliant. Usually made with pulverized and blanched almonds. In a product or as a paste, almond meal helps to unclog pores in the skin and absorb excess oil from skin. It can be used to make scrubs, lotions or cleansers.

**Aloe Vera Gel**: Aloe is renowned for its cooling, soothing, healing, nutritive and moisturizing qualities. The part of the aloe that's used comes from the juice inside the leaves of the aloe plant.

**Analgesic**: An ingredient or product that provides topical pain relief.

**Antioxidants**: Substances that inhibit oxidation, help depress rancidity and retard skin damage by environmental factors such as pollution. Some examples of natural antioxidants include vitamins A, C and E.

**Apple-Cider Vinegar**: A vinegar made from apples. Often used as a toner and pH adjuster (inside the body and out). Used in cooking, it has some tenderizing abilities. Also a great little cleaning clarifier.

**Apricot Kernel Oil**: An emollient and moisturizer pressed from the kernel of the apricot for penetrating and softening skin. It is non-greasy, has a high content of Vitamin E and can replace mineral oil. Mimics the skin's natural sebum and is readily absorbed into the skin. A great carrier oil as well. It has been used for millennia by the Hunza people contributing to their being the healthiest and longest-living people in the world.

**Apocrine and Eccrine Glands**: Sweat glands.

**Arnica**: Botanical. Anti-inflammatory skin protectant and bruise and discoloration inhibitor. From a plant containing healing and astringent properties, it is sometimes taken internally to help reduce bruising prior to cosmetic surgery. Germany's Commission E (Germany's equivalent to the United States FDA) has approved arnica for external use for injuries.

**Art Gum Eraser**: A crumbly eraser used by artists for fine-art drawing. Erases pencil and a few other things cleanly and completely.

**Astringent**: Ingredient that causes tightening and contraction of the pores and skin tissues. Also used to tone the skin.

**Avocado Oil**: A great skin moisturizer and luxurious massage oil, avocado was once known as an aphrodisiac.

**Baking Soda**: Also known as bicarbonate of soda (yes, the cooking kind). It is an absorbent and relieves itching and burning. Sometimes used for insect bites.

**Beeswax**: A beautiful, natural emollient that is soothing to the skin and an affordable product.

It is not a fragrant wax. It has a slightly warm honey smell. Used in older formulas for candles, cosmetics and furniture polish, it is used less often now because paraffin, a byproduct of petroleum, is less expensive.

**Bentonite Clay**: Porous clay from volcanic ash. It has been used in facial masks for tightening and firming the pores and as a thickener and stabilizer. It is made from silicate clay.

**Black Cohash Root**: Botanical. Once used by Native Americans, this plant has several uses associated with menopause and high blood pressure.

**Blue Vervain**: Botanical. Grown near swamps; also known as swamp verbena.

**Borax**: Known as 20 Mule Team® Borax, this laundry additive has been used for years in cosmetics for skin lightening, thickening and stabilization of products.

**Boric Acid**: Also known as orthoboric acid. A weak acid used both as an antiseptic for some skin conditions and as a mild insecticide.

**Botanical**: From the word botany; plants, algae and fungi.

**Bran**: From wheat bran, it is the fiber part of the kernel. It is a thickener and has calming properties to the skin.

**Calcium Carbonate**: A naturally occurring calcium salt found in limestone and coral; it has no known toxicity.

**Camphor**: Often used as an anesthetic and pain reliever. Its astringent, cooling properties also help with blood circulation. It is derived from a species of tree in the Orient that resembles the evergreen tree.

**Canola Oil**: Carrier or cooking oil and an emollient. It is extracted from rapeseed and is considered to be a natural replacement to mineral oil.

**Carrier**: Medium or base used for a preparation as a carrier for main ingredients or essential and fragrance oils. It works to "carry" the active ingredients which may have their own benefit as well.

**Castor Oil**: An oil from the seed of the castor bean plant. It is a very thick oil that will add richness and heaviness to a product.

**Chaste Tree Berry**: Tree berries that grow on shrubs, native to Croatia, but can be grown elsewhere.

**Chlordane**: A man-made pesticide.

**Citric Acid**: An acid full of wonderful AHAs that are good for your skin. It is also used as a buffer to help adjust the pH of products.

**Citronella**: Plant-based and used primarily in lotions, gels, and sprays as a natural bug repellent. Effective when combined with other natural essential oils that also repel insects and fleas.

**Clarify**: To balance the pH of the skin and remove residue from cleanser or other agents.

**Clay**: Usually sold as facial clay or French clay. This fine, white (also red) clay draws out oils and impurities from the skin. Also see betonite clay.

**Cocoa Butter**: An emollient, skin conditioner and skin protectant. It has a super-high mineral content, vitamin C and feel good "love" chemicals. Derived from the seeds of the cacao tree, it is extracted during the cocoa-making process. This is a solid, moisturizing and luxurious oil often used in making chocolate bars (gives the creamy consistency and form to the chocolate bar). Also a great alternative to petroleum jelly.

**Coconut Oil**: A natural antimicrobial, antifungal, antibacterial, antioxidant and anti-aging component. Coconut oil is the most stable oil known to man. It will not putrify or go rancid. Derived from the meat of the coconut, it is used in cosmetics as a very luxurious and wonderful skin moisturizer (I prefer coconut oil over petroleum jelly). Use it in place of petroleum jelly. Its smell will remind you of tropical suntan lotion.

**Dichloro-Diphenyl Trichloroethane (DDT)**: A toxic synthetic insecticide produced in the 1940s and so widely used that we still have traces in the earth and plants, etc. Now banned in some areas.

**Distilled Water**: Purified water through a distillation process (steam and heat process).

**Electrolytes**: Ions as "salts" that are electrically charged (naturally) to help your cells carry impulses through your body with nutrients.

**Emollient**: A substance that softens or smooths the surface of the skin.

**Emulsifier**: Ingredient that helps suspend two or more liquids that normally are not easily soluble to prevent separation.

**Exfoliate**: To loosen dead surface skin cells to expose new skin and a fresher smoother-looking skin surface.

**Free Radicals**: Damage to cells allowing molecules in the skin to be at risk of further damage.

**Ginger**: Sometimes shown as Hawaiian Awapuhi, it is a wonderful natural astringent, toner and clarifier.

**Glycerin**: Cream is to milk what glycerin is to fat. Glycerin comes from either animal or vegetable fat and it is very moisturizing. It actually draws moisture from the air right to your skin.

**Grape Seed Oil**: An antioxidant, carrier oil, emollient and moisturizer. It contains natural vitamin E and is good in massage oils. An amazing antioxidant for anti-aging benefits. One of the most nutritive oils known to man.

**Henna**: A natural skin and hair dye used for natural hair coloring and for making non-permanent long-lasting tattoos.

**Heptachlor**: A synthetic insecticide that was widely used; now, sometimes found in plants and animals.

**Herpes Simplex**: The form of herpes that produces cold sores.

**Honey**: Bees make this highly complex amazing elixir. It is an emollient, humectant, skin conditioner and hair conditioner.

**Humectant**: A substance (for example glycerin) that reduces water loss from the skin and aids in moisturizing; can sometimes pull moisture from air to skin.

**Jojoba Oil**: An emollient and moisturizer, it has a very high natural content of vitamin E. It is extremely skin nourishing and lasts longer in its natural state than most oils. Has been credited with skin healing. Provides rapid absorption.

**Kelp**: Sea kelp is full of trace minerals from the sea. It has nutritive value to skin and is used in Asia for soothing burns and rashes. Stimulating, revitalizing and nourishing to the skin due to its sulfur amino acid and iodine content. Kelp has anti-inflammatory and disinfectant properties. When harvested correctly, it is full of natural vitamins, minerals and enzymes.

**Lanolin**: This is the "sebum" from sheep skin. No harm is done to the animal; rather it is a byproduct of cleaning their wool. Sheep sebum is the closest to our own natural sebum and is sometimes used as a moisturizing ingredient.

**Lemon Juice**: A natural lightener for face and hair and a natural toner for the skin. Similar to apple-cider vinegar, lemon juice is great as a clarifier in cleaning products because of the acid content. Orange juice has similar uses.

**Lecithin**: A thick viscous material that occurs naturally. Found in eggs, animal and plant tissue; often used as an emulsifier.

**Lindane**: A neurotoxin that is used to treat scabies, head lice and crabs in people.

**Linseed Oil**: Usually found at the hardware store in the paint and stain section. It is used for wood finishing and in some furniture cleaners and polishes. It can be combustible and the fumes are strong, so mix in a well-ventilated area.

**Liquid Chlorophyll**: Green pigment found in plants and algae. A good system clarifier.

**Lye**: A harsh and dangerous acid made in the old days from rendering ashes from the fire. When used in soap making, lye goes through a process called saponification during the cooking process that changes the acid into a harmless alkaline.

**Lyme Disease**: A disease spread by ticks with a range of multiple bacterias that cause dangerous illness.

**Magnesium Sulfate**: A mineral mined from the earth.

**Melanin**: Found in human skin and hair it helps produce pigment.

**Melanocyte**: Pigment-producing skin cells that are in the bottom layer of the skins epidermis.

**Melatonin**: A naturally occurring hormone that assists in the regulation of rhythms for several biological functions.

**Motherwort**: Botanical. Member of the mint family with a wide range of uses.

**Olive Oil**: A lovely light-barrier and moisturizing oil rich in polyphenols and antioxidants. Hydrating and soothing to the skin, it often is used to help soothe burns and scrapes. In extra-pure form, called "sweet oil."

**Ozone Layer**: Formed above the earth's surface by the action of solar ultraviolet light. It helps work as a filter from the suns damaging rays.

**Papaya Enzyme**: Antioxidant. Contains a considerable amount of papain, folic acid, vitamin C, beta carotene and enzymes. Some antiseptic properties.

**Passionflower**: Botanical also known as passion vines or maypop. Sometimes used for medicinal purposes. As a tea, it can aid in relaxation and sleep.

**pH**: A measurement of how acidic or alkaline a product may be.

**Pomegranate**: Fruit with high antioxidants. Seeds are edible.

**Pure Essential Oils**: Essential oils that not only have therapeutic fragrances, but also contain countless varied compounds that facilitate healing and renewal for the skin and body. Pure food-grade essential oils used for millennia in many alternative healing traditions.

**Propylene Glycol**: Excluding water, this is the most common moisture-carrying substance used in cosmetic formulas; it leaves a non-greasy feel and is used often as a humectant; also serves as a solvent for antioxidants and preservatives. It can be an irritant at high concentrations, but is safe at levels of five percent or lower.

**Propolis**: Bees collect a substance from the buds of trees resembling resin. They convert this resin into propolis. This flavonoid-rich substance has both anti-inflammatory and antiseptic properties, working also as an anti-toxin. It is a germ-resistant coating.

**Safflower Oil**: Used in cooking, this oil provides emollients to the skin and can be used as a carrier oil.

**Sebaceous**: Small glands in the skin that secrete sebum (the skin's natural oil).

**Shea Butter**: An anti-inflammatory, emollient and humectant from an African tree, this popular butter is used as a rich moisturizer, super skin protectant and lubricant.

**Solubilizer**: Solubilizes, usually into aqueous vehicles, normally insoluble material; examples include fragrances, oils, etc.

**Soy Wax**: Made from soy. You can substitute it in most recipes calling for beeswax.

**Sun Protection Factor (SPF)**: An instrument of measurement by which a lab can determine the sunscreen effectiveness.

**Subcutaneous Layer**: A layer of fat between the skin and muscles.

**Sweet Almond Oil**: An emollient and moisturizer; a natural vegetable oil pressed from almonds used for penetrating and softening. Massage therapists have long used this moisturizing oil for massage. It is used to soften dry skin, help relieve dry, itchy and irritated skin and it is used in cosmetics.

**Sweet Oil**: A pure form of olive oil; see olive oil.

**Tea Tree Oil**: A toner with antibacterial and antimicrobial properties, as well as an anti-inflammatory. Natural antiseptic. It is also known as melaleuca oil.

**Tincture**: To extract an herb or other plant material and place in alcohol for concentrated preservation.

**Titanium Dioxide**: From natural mineral salts and used for lightening a product.

**UVA**: Ultraviolet rays that are long-range solar rays from the sun.

**UVB**: Short-wave solar rays from the sun.

**Valerian Root**: Botanical. Shows effectiveness as a calmative to promote relaxation and sleep.

**Vegetable Shortening/Vegetable Oil**: An oil usually used for frying or baking (loaded with fats and calories when used internally). It creates great external lubrication. Vegetable oils are very inexpensive and give good results for combating dry skin. Consider these a petroleum-free Vaseline® replacement. Cheaper and more natural.

**Vermiculite**: A natural substance from minerals that expands with heat and water; an absorbent.

**Viscosity**: Refers to the thickness and degree of pourability or stickiness of a product; high viscosity is very thick, like a hand cream or honey, and low viscosity is readily pourable and thin like water.

**Volatile Organic Compound (VOC)**: Volatile organic compound. Hydrocarbons are emitted gasses from certain solids that vaporize in the atmosphere and add damage to the ozone layer around the earth.

**Water Soluble**: Will dissolve in water.

**Wild Yam**: Botanical. Known by several names; has long been used for menopausal symptoms.

**Witch Hazel**: A great natural replacement for traditional alcohol. Also used as an anti-inflammatory, astringent and a botanical.

**Zinc Oxide**: Inorganic compound; not water soluble; reflects the sun's rays.

# RECIPE INDEX

# RESOURCES

Most of the items in this book can be found on the Internet and in your local grocery, health food, pharmacy or hardware stores.

# ABOUT THE AUTHOR

Casey Kellar is a well-known industry professional, a national speaker for business development, author of five books on natural toiletries, skin care, fragrances, spa products, natural remedies and natural products for home, garden and pets in addition to being a wife, mother and grandmother.

Founder and former CEO of RainShadow Labs and RainCountry Naturals, Casey has been involved with the beauty and home fragrance business industry for over 23 years. She has created over 500 formulas as a "natural" chemical designer and compounder for the skin care, cleaning and home fragrance industries. As a consultant for more than 3,000 companies worldwide, Casey has developed products for such names as L'Oreal®, Nike®, and many others.

Casey enjoys spending time with her husband, Byron, and traveling between their homes in Hawaii and Long Beach, Washington.

# METRIC TABLE

## WEIGHT (OR MASS)

| Imperial Unit | Metric Unit | Metric Unit | Imperial Unit |
|---|---|---|---|
| Ounce | 28.35 grams | Gram | 0.035 ounces |
| Pound | 0.45 kilograms | Kilogram | 2.21 pounds |
| UK ton (2240 pounds) | 1.02 metric tons | Metric ton (1000kg) | 0.98 UK tons |
| US ton (2000 pounds) | 0.91 tons | Metric ton (1000kg) | 1.10 US tons |

## AREA

| Imperial Unit | Metric Unit | Metric Unit | Imperial Unit |
|---|---|---|---|
| Acre | 0.40 hectare | Hectare | 2.47 acres |
| Square inch | 6.45 square centimeters | Square centimeter | 0.16 square inches |
| Square foot | 0.09 square meters | Square Meter | 1.20 square yard |
| Square yard | 0.84 square meters | Square kilometer | 0.39 square miles |
| Square mile | 2.60 square kilometers | Cubic meter | 35.23 cubic feet |
| Cubic foot | 0.028 cubic meters | Cubic meter | 1.35 cubic yards |
| Cubic yard | 0.76 cubic meters | | |

## TEMPERATURE

| | |
|---|---|
| °C = (°F - 32) ÷ 1.8 | For example: (68°F - 32) ÷ 1.8 = (36) ÷ 1.8 = 20°C |
| °F = (°C x 1.8) + 32 | For example: (20°C x 1.8) + 32 = (36) + 32 = 68°F |

# VOLUME

| Imperial Unit | Metric Unit | Metric Unit | Imperial Unit |
|---|---|---|---|
| Teaspoon (UK) | 5.92 milliliters | Millilitre | 0.17 teaspoons (UK) |
| Teaspoon (US) | 4.93 milliliters | Millilitre | 0.20 teaspoons (US) |
| Tablespoon (UK) | 17.76 milliliters | 10 Millilitre | 0.56 tablespoons (UK) |
| Tablespoon (US) | 14.79 milliliters | 10 Millilitre | 0.68 tablespoons (US) |
| Fluid ounce (UK) | 28.41 milliliters | 100 Millilitre | 3.52 fluid ounces (UK) |
| Fluid ounce (US) | 29.57 milliliters | 100 Millilitre | 3.38 fluid ounces (US) |
| Pint (UK) | 0.57 liters | Liter | 1.76 pints (UK) |
| Pint (US) | 0.47 liters | Liter | 2.11 pints (US) |
| Quart (UK) | 1.14 liters | Liter | 0.88 quarts (UK) |
| Quart (US) | 0.95 liters | Liter | 1.06 quarts (US) |
| Gallon (UK) | 4.55 liters | Liter | 0.22 gallon (UK) |
| Gallon (US) | 3.79 liters | Liter | 0.26 gallon (US) |

# PRESSURE

| Imperial Unit | Metric Unit | Metric Unit | Imperial Unit |
|---|---|---|---|
| 1 pound per square inch (psi) | 6894.76 Pascal (Pa=N/m$^2$) | 10,000 Pascal (Pa=N/m$^2$) | 1.45 pound per square inch (psi) |
| 1 pound per square inch (psi) | 6.90 kilopascal (kN/m$^2$) | 10 kilopascal (kN/m$^2$) | 1.45 pound per square inch (psi) |
| 1 pound per square inch (psi) | 0.69 bar | 0.1 bar | 1.45 pound per square inch (psi) |